LEARNING AND TEACHING THROUGH ART AND CRAFTS

LEARNING AND TEACHING THROUGH ART AND CRAFTS

ALAN COTTON AND
FRANK HADDON

B T BATSFORD LIMITED   LONDON

First published 1974
ISBN 0 7134 2825 2

Designed by Mark Gerlings, Libra Studios
Set in 10/11 pt Monophoto Erhardt 453
by Keyspools Limited, Golborne
Printed and bound in Great Britain by
Wm Clowes and Sons Limited, Beccles, Suffolk
for the publishers
B T Batsford Limited
4 Fitzhardinge Street, London W1H 0AH

CONTENTS

ACKNOWLEDGMENT

The authors would like to express their gratitude to the many children with whom they have worked and to students and colleagues in the Art Department of Rolle College who have contributed to the work and ideas in this book.

A very special thanks must go to the following:
Mervyn Williams and staff at Withycombe Raleigh Primary School, Exmouth; Reg Mear and staff at Newton St Cyres Primary School, Devon; Mark Lear and staff at Exeter Road Primary School, Exmouth; Reg Chapman and staff at Exmouth Church Primary School, Exmouth; Edna King and staff at Littleham Infant School, Exmouth; G J W Joyce and the art staff at Sidmouth School, Sidmouth.

Grateful thanks are also due to Harriet Murray-Browne, Craft Editor for B T Batsford, for her invaluable help.

Photographs were taken by the authors and Howard Jones, and Alan Gentle and Felicity Green of the A V A Department, Rolle College.

INTRODUCTION

It is more important for a teacher to have some understanding of the role of art in education and its meaning for the child than to have specific skills in, say, pottery or weaving or painting. Such an understanding, however, cannot be achieved in a vacuum; some experience of materials and the problems of making images is necessary. This book is concerned with specific activities, with processes and skills, but also aims by demonstrating what learning is involved to justify their place in the curriculum, and to show how they are related to general educational objectives. We are attempting to provide a rationalé for art teaching and to offer principles upon which a teacher can design an appropriate programme of activities.

Nothing that is said here is intended to devalue the intuitive, spontaneous interaction of the teacher with the children, for it is the ability to respond with insight to the needs of children (and the opportunities of the moment) which is the hallmark of the outstanding teacher. There is no opposition between this flexible approach and planning. Given some overall objectives many activities can be seen as contributing towards their achievement, and teaching can become purposeful, directional and sequential without the loss of spontaneity and responsiveness.

Without aesthetic experience a child or a man is to a certain extent deprived. Aesthetic experience covers a wide range of activities – music, drama, poetry, dance, literature, to name but the most obvious, and each has its own contribution to make to the education of the child. The visual arts, however, offer a unique contribution, providing experience of making images and of using materials through which the child may develop a language with which to 'model' his interaction with the world.

We have not attempted to cover all the possible activities within this field. There are many books to which teachers can refer for information about processes and techniques; we are concerned with providing a basis upon which a teacher or student can choose which activities to introduce and develop. A continual pursuit of new activities is to be avoided, since it can mean children are often working at a superficial level. In such situations there is little connection between one activity and another and little sequential learning is likely to occur. Our intention, therefore, is to encourage the development of a thoughtful approach to the curriculum which looks primarily for the educational value in various art activities, and seeks something more than enjoyment or an end product which may look impressive in a display.

Such an attitude also raises another important issue. In many schools the various activities which are grouped loosely under the umbrella term of art and crafts have ceased to exist in their own right and arise out of topic and project work – largely as an illustration service. This again makes it difficult to plan any proper sequence of activities and may lead to a somewhat haphazard collection of art experiences for a child. Topic or project work is undoubtedly valuable, but if art is limited exclusively to work arising in such a way, a child's education in this field is likely to be severely restricted.

Most pupils will cease to become makers of art as soon as they leave school, yet much of our art education is devoted to practical activities with little regard for the development of critical or appreciative skills and knowledge. An important component of art education should be the development of a response to art in its widest sense. This will involve some knowledge of western art and its history and some understanding of the role that art has occupied in different cultures. Art education in the past has paid too much attention to motivating the child to produce art, and too little attention to what concept of art the child was developing. Yet the work that a child produces and his attitude towards the subject as a whole will be dependent on this fundamental concept.

The section that follows introduces some basic ideas about art in general education and the role of the teacher. The remainder of the book is devoted to a more detailed examination of various aspects of art work. For convenience this is divided into two- and three-dimensional work, although not all activities fall neatly into the two categories. These chapters are supported by a series of illustrations which show more clearly than words how children work. There is also a section on art and the backward child, and a bibliography and an appendix give information on further reading, materials and processes.

Art in education

So much goes on under the banner of 'art' that any comprehensive definition is impossible. It is possible, however, to offer a working definition of art as far as children are concerned. Their approach to art is essentially the artist's traditional approach of making images or pictures. Usually the central concern of the artist has been the making of pictures or sculptures which represented some aspect of the world as he knew it. Children also make models of their world – but it is a world of feeling and ideas, not the visual world seen with adult eyes. Hence what they draw and paint has all the distortion and simplicity which arises from the subjectivity of the children's thinking and their comparative lack of knowledge.

'A work of art is not reality: it is a model of reality. It is a play on reality. It is a toy. We are able to play with it; we are able to play around it with ideas: we come to understand it and through it to understand reality.'
Painting: some basic principles   Frederick Gore

'Model' sounds a grand term for the simple painting a child makes of his mother or even for the studies made by older children or adults, but in fact that is just what they are. Certain aspects of a subject are abstracted and made into a drawing or painting. In modelling reality we are, in fact, discovering it, for the process is one of sorting out experience and coming to understand it. Art is like play in that it is an activity in which various versions of reality are

tested out to see which is the best 'fit' to the experience that has prompted the act of painting or drawing.

The visual arts offer a mode of expression which is predominately personal – what is produced will be unique to the individual producing it. It is the result of a personal response to an experience or an idea, expressed through a personal response to particular materials and processes. Visual arts, and other art forms too, offer this very special opportunity to assert our individuality. The careful fostering of personal qualities in the work of children is one of the fundamental tasks of the teacher and should rank high among his objectives.

Freedom

For many years the idea of 'free expression' has dominated much of art teaching, and teachers have been reluctant to encroach on the freedom of the child by offering suggestions or teaching skills to him. At the same time teachers have been a little disappointed with the results of such an approach. The truth is that a child is not made free by the removal of restrictions or direction, but thrown back on his own undeveloped powers and personal resources, which are often inadequate. Freedom is the power to do what you want to do. The role of the teacher is to help the child gain such power. This is a complex task. It demands a delicate balance between leaving the child alone to explore some new idea or process, and coming in with help and suggestions, with the danger of over-directing the child and destroying the very qualities of self-initiative which the teacher is trying to foster.

No teacher should be afraid to put new opportunities before children, or to give them clear instruction on how to begin exploring the materials that are provided. What is essential is that a process should be taught in such a way that it opens up a range of possibilities, and is not restricted to one result. For example: the technique of coiling a clay pot can be taught as just that – a technique for making a pot. But it is much more than that; it is a technique for making hollow forms, and so it can be used to make pots or pieces of sculpture. It is important that the child realises that he has a technique at his command which can be used in a variety of ways to suit his purposes, and that it can be used in conjunction with the other basic clay techniques of slab building and making hollow forms by pinching or throwing. Reference to the section on printing will provide other examples of this open-ended approach where a technique is introduced in principle for the child to explore and develop in his own way.

The nature of choice

Merely to provide a range of materials is to court disappointment, for choice without experience of the materials and tools available is not real choice, it is only picking at random. Some children in this situation continue to use what they are already familiar with, and teachers complain of the children's lack of enterprise and their general inhibition. Real choice is based on experience of what is offered, and it is vital that the teacher, from time to time, deliberately restricts the children's choice so that they all gain experience of some particular medium or process. Periods of structured experience can then alternate with opportunities to choose freely among the available possibilities, and in this way real choice, and therefore proper responsibility, can be exercised. As in all the other areas, the concern of the primary teacher should be in building attitudes, and the techniques are important in so far as they provide the means by which attitudes can be developed.

Art in the general curriculum

If, as so often happens, the school is working on an integrated pattern in which there are no lessons (except for the subjects requiring particular facilities such as PE or music) it may be difficult for the teacher to ensure that the children have basic art experiences. This is especially true if art is relegated to the role of an illustration service to other subject areas.

Projects on 'The Post Office' or 'Transport through the Ages' or any other of the common topics to be found in primary schools, if the main approach is through reading and copying from books, provide very little basis for genuine art work – one might add that they provide very little basis for any other sort of learning either. This is not an attack on children using books for research, but real learning occurs when children have to respond to genuine first-hand experience, or to give order and meaning to data they have themselves collected. Whatever the theme, this principle of providing some direct experience is essential if children are expected to work seriously and meaningfully in art.

The teacher's role

The teacher's role has been implicit in all that has been written previously. Essentially it is:

a   to act as technical adviser helping to solve practical problems
d   to be the initiator of activities through the provision of understand what he is attempting to do
c   to provide materials and opportunities
d   to be the initiator of activities through the provision of appropriate stimuli
e   to develop a climate of opinion in the classroom in which art has a high value

This could be called the teacher's tactical role, but there is also a strategic role. This is concerned with defining objectives and planning the curriculum through which those objectives can be achieved; with evaluating the teaching and learning over a period of time; with assessing the needs of the children and the resources available, and relating objectives and curriculum to these. The real task of the teacher, having set out aims and objectives, is to translate these into actual activities which are appropriate to individual children, for if art is to lay claim to anything it must be to the value of the individual effort. Teachers in primary schools and in middle schools, because of their continuous contact with their children, are able to build up an intimate knowledge of each child in their class and are in a position to diagnose the needs of individuals and to make plans on this basis.

The subject itself provides objectives in terms of increasingly complex concepts or skills. From knowledge of the subject, the teacher can decide what is an appropriate starting point for children, and will have some ideas about how to build on the simple beginning to reach more complex and difficult stages of work. There is, of course, choice about what is the best starting point. Children can be introduced to printing through mono-printing or through printing with junk. The first stage in work with textiles can be junk printing or tie-dyeing. The decision depends on facilities, the teacher's skill and preference and, above all, on knowledge of the children's needs and their likely response to a particular approach. This in turn will be based on their previous experience and the connections between what is envisaged and other areas of work being currently pursued.

If, for example, children of eleven are using colour straight from the palettes and are satisfied with the limited range of colours provided, then their 'need' is for experience of colour mixing and work based on some starting point which would make use of such experience. A study of a local street would provide an opportunity to observe the colours of different types of walls. Children's attention could be drawn to the staining resulting from rusty iron pipes letting water run down a wall, or perhaps drips from copper roofing staining a bright green-blue. The concrete cappings to gate pillars are often covered with yellow lichens, and where these have died they leave a subtle patina of ash greys. Brick walls provide an astonishing range of browns and reds; the cement or mortar yet another range of subtle changes if the wall is old and has been patched and re-pointed many times.

If the teacher has a clear grasp of overall objectives then he can diagnose the children's needs and find opportunities to set up the right sort of experiences for them. Any project can be examined to see what special opportunities it offers for achieving his objectives. With another class with different needs the same village street could provide opportunities to study pattern or textures, or perhaps the shapes of chimney pots could be the basis for making a range of slab and coil pots. Almost every topic or project offers a wide range of starting points and what will be selected depends very much on the teacher's long term plans. This does not mean that the teacher is always imposing his ideas and directing what children shall do; it does mean that he will use all the skill at his disposal to turn children's interest and enthusiasm to those things which are likely to be the most profitable and of long term benefit to them.

Criteria of suitability

There are many things that children can do and many books giving technical advice on how to do them: the real problem is to decide what is worthwhile offering to children and worthwhile investing time, money and energy in pursuing. It is impossible to give a set answer, for this will depend on the children and their previous experience, the knowledge and enthusiasm of the teacher and the resources available in the school. It is possible, however, to lay down certain criteria which can be summed up briefly.

Can the children do it successfully?
Will they do it enthusiastically?
Is it worthwhile doing?

Many activities meet the first two of these simple criteria but fail to meet the third and crucial test. Sticking shells around jam jars is a typical example. Drawing round templates or using tracings are other common activities which also fail this test. There is no point in doing things which have little educational value although there may be occasions when the teacher resorts to simple activities of the sort denigrated in order to get particularly difficult or backward children involved in some sort of activity from which more creative work may evolve.

The teacher and creativity

Creative learning is fostered by creative teachers who are able to see the significance of the unplanned opportunity and pounce upon it as something to develop and elaborate. Such an opportunity must, however, have some bearing upon an interest or enquiry for it to be seen as significant:

'surprise is the privilege only of prepared minds – minds with structured expectancies and interests.'
The Conditions of Creativity Bruner J S

Objectives and planning also imply both for the teacher and the child a sense of value in what is being done, for the teacher cannot help but transmit her purposefulness in her teaching and her confidence in what she is doing.

At the root of creativity, whether it be the teacher's or the child's, is the feeling of confidence. For the child this depends on his sense of personal security and his estimation of himself. This is largely built upon other people's estimation of him, which is transmitted to him continuously by his parents, his teacher and his fellow pupils. This is why the attitude of the teacher is so important, for in the highly controlled situation of the school his estimation of the child largely determines the child's estimation of himself *in the learning situation*. If the teacher, and particularly the teacher of the younger children whose attitudes are to some extent unformed, can enter into the child's thinking, if he is prepared to let work develop in unexpected directions according to the child's needs and interests, if he can find and express genuine pleasure in what the child does, then a creative relationship is being formed. It is on this basis that the child can develop confidence and move towards that personal autonomy which is one of the great goals of education. This does not mean that a teacher should not influence children – the whole purpose of this book is to show just how teachers can and should influence children – but he should be highly aware of how he is influencing them and particularly of the pattern of values which are active in his classroom. He has the major responsibility for these, and through the way they operate he is responsible for the growth or the erosion of the child's creative ability.

DRAWING AND PAINTING

For the young child drawing provides a natural, pictorial language which he uses to express his feelings and to communicate his relationship with the world. For the older child many vague ideas can be explored and clarified through the process of drawing. It can be used to investigate structure, function, form and scale, through the examination and recording of objects or aspects of the environment. Drawings can range from the most objective, diagrammatic statement of function to the most subjective, personal expression (see figure 1). The art of drawing can heighten perception, give greater understanding and enable a child to give his experiences an ordered form.

Early experiences

The beginnings of drawing occur early in the child's life even before he can scribble. Before he can talk a child will make marks by dipping his fingers in custard or gravy and patting or pushing it around the table. A little later he explores what marks can be made with puddles of water, or will scratch into mud or sand. Given paper and crayons he will scribble.

In these early stages a child is not making images but discovering that he can obtain a record of his physical action. Early attempts show little evidence of visual control. The scribble tends to go off the paper and to be unrelated to its size.

The speed with which development takes place and the age at which it occurs vary very much, and clearly one important factor is the extent to which the child is encouraged by adults and provided with materials and the opportunity for discovery. From around the age of one, children can be given cheap paper – wrapping papers, old wallpaper, thin drawing paper, newsprint or kitchen paper and pastels, crayons, coloured pencils, felt-tipped pens or

1   *The bride* by a four year old girl

brushes and liquid paints to work with. If these basic requirements are met and the child provided with a place where he can work freely without mess being a source of trouble, he will go to such activity whenever he feels the need for it.

The development of images

Images develop from the early primitive forms that the child makes in his scribbling and he will give names to what he has 'drawn'. This is not an entirely natural development; it usually stems from an adult, being faced with the child's scribble, asking what it is, and the child responding by calling it 'Daddy' or whatever is uppermost in his mind. This is an important development, for it establishes for the child that he can communicate through drawing and that *his* marks on paper have significance and can 'stand for' something else. He has entered into a symbolic activity which, for a few years, may be of very great importance to him.

The early drawings of children show their concern with the everyday things and events around them. They draw their families, houses, pets, weddings, the arrival of new cars – anything, in fact which has significance for them. They draw their experiences, *not what they see*. This is a vital point for the understanding and enjoyment of children's drawings and paintings. Their drawings are symbols which stand for their experience and they depict therefore, what they know. Children's experience is largely visual but they have not learnt to see as adults see, nor does their ability to symbolise their experience keep pace always with the demands they make upon it. The drawings of children in the infants school are characterised by their experimental and changing nature. Children change and develop the symbols they use, and even in one drawing may exhibit different symbols for, say, man.

At first, the child's capacity to create visual symbols is limited because he lacks the control necessary to make clearly differentiated forms. His 'vocabulary' may be little more than a rough circle which he will use in different sizes to convey the information he wants to communicate.

Another important characteristic of young children's work is their inability to depict the relationships between the 'bits' of information they are drawing. The child knows that a man has eyes, hair and teeth but he is unable to relate these items in a way which has any resemblance to their actual relationships. It is only gradually as a child's grasp of such relationships develops that they begin to appear in his pictorial work. Any collection of drawings from an infant class will reveal wide differences between children of similar ages in this respect, and if one looks, for example, at the placing of arms in relation to body it is clear that children's grasp of this relationship is very varied.

The emergence of schemata

For most children, usually towards the age of seven, but depending very much on the opportunities they have had for drawing and painting and the encouragement they have received, the culmination of the experimenting is the emergence of a set of schemata for the things they commonly draw – the human figure, houses, cars, trees, flowers, the sun, animals. The list will vary from child to child, but the schemata are essentially personal symbols which are used in a consistent manner. The schema which a child develops for woman, for example, will appear in basically similar form in all his drawings. It can be regarded as a basic formula which can be modified in detail to fit particular needs. The same schema may be used to depict mother and daughter but it will be modified by a change of scale and differences in detail of clothing, hair style and other items which are of significance to the child in distinguishing one from the other. Once the schemata emerge, development is then essentially their steady refinement so that they carry more and more information and are more clearly differentiated to meet specific requirements. Accompanying the development of the individual schemata, there is also an increasing awareness of the actual relationships between the objects they depict. These too are more precisely expressed although, again, the child's symbolism for spatial relationships may seem far from correct to adult eyes.

The typical child's drawing shows figures, house and tree standing on a strip of brown representing ground, with another strip of blue across the top of the paper representing sky. Again, this shows the world as the child knows it to be, rather than as it appears. The use of the ground-line gives way later to another convention for depicting space in which the child sets out his figures and objects – houses, trees, tractors, and so on – spread across a plane. This gives to adult eyes the impression of an aerial view, for in this version the sky has either disappeared altogether or has become a narrow band of blue at the top of the paper. Sometimes an intermediate stage separates these two, and a picture will contain two or more base-lines in the child's attempt to express objects or events which take place in depth. Yet another illustration of this adherence to knowledge rather than appearance is shown in the 'x-ray'

2 A painting by an infant after a visit to the zoo

adult logic, and this he cannot do. Under such pressure children will pick up tricks of drawing without understanding – they will, for example, obligingly paint the sky until it touches the ground line, but their lack of understanding is demonstrated by the way they will paint the sky round and underneath objects, such as houses, leaving them, as it were, suspended in the sky. Any pressure on a child to change his way of expressing his ideas is likely to be harmful, in that it undermines his confidence in his own ability.

The role of the teacher

The child's drawing changes and develops as he grows in experience. The richer the range of first-hand experiences he has, the richer will be the images he creates. His work will develop because he has more to say and he must alter and elaborate his schemata to carry more information. It is true that he will be increasingly aware of how other children are expressing their ideas, and he cannot help being influenced by this and the illustrations he sees in books and magazines. If, however, he is not under pressure to conform to any particular way of expressing himself, there is some chance that he will select only those ways which are pertinent to his needs. The teacher has a two-fold role in this respect. He should provide the child with as much authentic experience as he can – looking at and handling the things that interest and excite him, moving out into the local environment of the school to seek starting points in colour and texture and pattern, generating excitement and affection for the everyday things of the world around. Secondly, he can ensure that the work which is put up in the room shows many ways of expression, so that no one particular way is implied to be *the* way of drawing and painting. The child can also be shown how artists, both of other ages and our own, have found ways of saying what they want to say which are different from the conventional realism which is so often thought to be the 'right' way.

What is often termed 'imaginative' work is frequently based on memory images, derived not from personal experience on the part of the child but from illustrations in books and magazines or from films and television. The imaginative artist, however, usually works from visual

drawing. Children see nothing wrong in showing both the inside and the outside of a house if what they want to say can best be expressed in this way.

It is beyond the scope of this book to set down all the schematic stages that a child goes through in his development. Detailed documentation of these can be found in the specialist books listed in the bibliography, but it is important for the teacher to recognise that these changes are a natural part of the child's development and that they occur for all normal children. Although one cannot set down particular ages, for each stage the *sequence* of stages seems to be constant.

Any attempt to challenge the child over the way he draws, to suggest that he is wrong and should draw things in a different way in conformity with adult conventions, is to ask him to see through adult eyes and to reason with experience which is recorded immediately in some way and then later modified, recombined, or abstracted from, to form a new work. For example, the Italian paintings of the Renaissance are in every sense 'imaginative' but they are based on many objective studies of the figure, plants, landscape and architecture. Whilst it might not be appropriate for children to go through the full process of recording and then working from such studies, their imaginary work should stem from a rich sensory experience. The teacher's function is to provide stimulation, usually of a visual type, and to help the child to organise his imagery in such a way that he derives satisfaction and benefit from the activity. It may well be that sometimes this is achieved by focusing the child's attention on something that has taken place outside the school or by inviting him to revive memories of past experience. Marion Richardson's word pictures, which were based on the everyday scenes that her girls saw around the school in Dudley, are a good example of this latter approach. They were effective because they drew upon images which were there in the girls' minds waiting to be evoked.

Starting points for creative work
Visual starting points are basically of two kinds:

1   The objective
In this category come all those things which are studied for what they *are*. They offer interesting, exciting, pleasurable, novel experiences because of their shape, form, texture, colour and all the associations that go with these qualities. A full list would be endless, but in this category come flowers, driftwood, skulls, things seen under the magnifying glass or microscope, bits of machinery, fruits, insects – anything which can excite a response. Also in this category come all those things which can be studied outside the classroom; trees, buildings, cliffs, quarries, industrial landscapes, the sea-shore. Every environment has its own particular range of opportunities and one should not forget the special possibilities offered by museums and zoos. Figures 2 and 3 show paintings by a group of infants after a visit to an animal house where the children had been able to handle the animals and ask questions about them. Such

3   A painting by an infant after a visit to the zoo

discussion served to heighten the children's awareness of the special characteristics of the different animals and provided opportunities for other lines of investigation. Figure 4 is an example of work by a nine year old child at school. In this case the children were taken for a walk around the streets near their school after a preparatory discussion in which the teacher talked about the things they might see – chimney pots, unusual shapes for windows and doors, the materials used for walls and roofs, how roofs were treated at the top. The area around the school was particularly rich in Victorian and Edwardian houses which provided very good examples of rich decoration in wall treatment, ridge tiles, gable ends, fanlights – many details that the children had walked by each day without seeing. On their return they were asked to draw buildings which were imaginary but based on what they had seen. If the example shown is

4   A drawing by a nine year old child after a walk around
the streets near his school

compared with the usual drawing of a house by a child of
this age it is clear that a great deal has been observed and
has been used to enrich the child's concepts of a house.

The same class a little later was taken out to look at
another street and asked to make drawings on the spot.
There were two follow-up pieces of work from these; each
child made a small lino-cut which was printed in black ink

on white paper as a simple Christmas card; and secondly,
each child constructed a collage of a house from his drawing. All the collages were then put together to form a large
wall-decoration of a street. When the individual collages
had been assembled in this way, various members of the
class made people, trees, cars and other items to add to the
deserted street. The finished product was 'imaginary' but it

stemmed from, and was enriched by, the initial experience of studying the houses in the street near the school.

2 *The evocative or imaginative*

In this category come those things which are studied not for what they are, but because they stimulate ideas and images. They require an imaginative act on the part of the child and aim to arouse feelings and to awaken images of previous experience. Typical examples might be a sheet thrown over a group of objects to suggest a snow-covered mountain, or a box with holes cut in it to represent windows and lit by torches from inside. If the latter can be viewed in a darkened room, the effect is not unlike a building at night or on fire, and figure 5 was produced by this type of stimulus.

Such 'models' allow the child to visualise a personal interpretation and to select a viewpoint to develop accordingly. Discussion helps to focus the child's attention on relevant parts of the experience and draws attention to visual facts. In the case of the illuminated box the contrast of the dark walls seen against the light interior was an important piece of visual information.

Children themselves can make the models. Many boys are interested in model cars, trains and aeroplanes, and objects they can make up from plastic model kits. Figure 6 shows a drawing made by a boy after making a model of a train going over a bridge. The detailed observation of the engine made by this nine year old boy is evidence both of his involvement in the subject and of the capacity children have for making beautiful, informative drawings when they are really interested. Girls also have interests which can be tapped in this way, for instance dolls and the miniature doll's house.

In these last suggestions the distinction between the two categories of starting point becomes somewhat blurred. The boy who drew his model engine was being as objective as when he sat in the street and drew the strange shapes to be found on a local building. However, the bridge under the engine and the banks were books and boxes, and his imagination was required to transform these objects into a suitable setting for his train.

The work of young children will not necessarily show evidence of recent visual experience, but such experience may none-the-less be valuable and provide opportunities

5 *The fire* by a thirteen year old boy

for discussion with the teacher or with other children. As children move up through the primary school they need more stimulus and respond enthusiastically to studying the world around them. Drawing and painting becomes not only an expressive activity but a learning experience in which they explore what is being studied and record factual information. This does not exclude the expressive component of the activity which lies in the personal style of the drawing or painting. The initial selection of subject and viewpoint can also be a matter of personal decision.

If the drawings of ten year olds are compared with those of seven year olds, the differences often lie in the amount of information conveyed, the control with which the work is executed, the subtlety and variety of colour and the references to specific experience or ideas. Typically, however, the ten year old's drawing is still essentially schematic. Figure 7 gives clear evidence of this, for despite the amount of detailed information that the child has attempted to con-

6 A drawing by a nine year old boy after making a
model of a train going over a bridge

7 A painting by a ten year old child

vey, he is still not truly concerned with visual appearances as they actually are at a given moment. Children of this age are not concerned with light and shade or with accidents of colour, or with perspective except in a very simple way, nor with changes of colour arising through distance. In a similar way their attempts to convey movement are schematic rather than realistic; a group of running figures will all be in much the same position, all probably seen from one side.

The photographic image

We live, however, in a world which is dominated visually by the photographic image, and as children move through the junior school they become increasingly aware of the differences between their schematic imagery and pictures in books and magazines which are more 'real'. Their confidence is easily undermined and they begin to doubt their ability to draw. The problem is that to draw realistically it is necessary to forget what is known of the nature of things, and to find out how they actually appear from a particular point of view, at a particular time in a particular light. Take the classroom with white painted metal window frames; if the class is asked 'what colour are the window frames?' they will answer truthfully 'white'. But seen against the sky at mid-day they will appear a dark grey, seen late in a winter afternoon with the light on in the classroom they will probably appear a warm cream. Unless we are asked 'what colour do they actually appear to be?' we always answer what we know to be the unchanging 'real' colour. This is the crux of the problem, for which is 'real' – the appearance of an object or its unchanging characteristics? Realistic or naturalist painting to a very large extent only exists by capturing the fleeting appearances of the visual world and so for the child this means abandoning what he knows and pursuing what he can actually see. For many children this is too difficult a process and if they continue to draw and paint it is through the adoption of some formula which they can apply without much reference to actuality. Painting at GCE and CSE level is often of this kind, and is pathetically devoid of any evidence of looking at the world outside the classroom.

Overcoming lack of confidence

There are two ways of dealing with this problem. Firstly, since children have spent years acquiring and perfecting schemata for the everyday things of their world, it is far more likely that they will draw with a fresh vision if they are presented with objects which are new to them, objects for which they have no schema that has to be suppressed in order to draw more objectively. There is a great deal of material of this sort. Minute objects seen through a magnifying glass or microscope are strange and new and require children to draw in a precise, controlled manner which they find satisfying. Any object which the child can hold in his hand or put on the desk close to him to study is likely to lead to good drawing, providing it is intrinsically interesting for him because of qualities of colour, texture or form, or because of the associations it has for him. By good drawing we mean that the child has been involved in the act of drawing and has been able to convey information about the object under study in a way that is satisfying to him. If a child's confidence in his ability to draw can be built up through this approach, then he is better equipped to tackle more ambitious projects based on the environment around the school or at the local museum, for example. Again, it is essential that the child's interest is aroused in the subject matter itself, and the most potent influence here is the teacher's own enthusiasm. Certain things have an immediate appeal for most children, eg birds and animals, but with skill and enthusiasm a teacher can awaken children's interest in less obvious material. Schools which are set on steep hills in towns, for example, may offer vistas of roofs which are rich in texture and colour; country schools are near to farms, woods and fields.

The task of listing all the possibilities of each sort of area would be endless, but some mention should be made of what is probably the bleakest environment from this particular point of view – the housing estate. Here the school may be surrounded by many streets of similar modern houses with few established trees, no fields, no natural hedges, no old buildings. Efforts can be made to go further afield for starting points but this is impracticable for much of the time, and it is essential that the teacher begins to build resources in the classroom. These can include many sorts of attractive objects – stuffed birds, driftwood, plants, aquariums, classroom animals – the interests of the teacher and the general direction of work in the classroom will govern the bias of the collection, which will vary from term to term. The idea of a collection is not new, particularly for infant teachers who have had their nature tables and interest corners for many years, except insofar as this collection will be particularly biased towards visual qualities. However, the environment of the housing estate may not be completely lacking in possibilities, although these may be of a transitory nature and require that the teacher seizes opportunities when they present themselves. A street can be transformed by a sudden burst of low sunshine after heavy rain, when houses, cars and people become dark shapes against dazzling silver surfaces. Similarly, on days of heavy showers and sunshine, houses may appear brilliantly illuminated against a dark sky or set under a rainbow. Sunrise and sunset, snow, frost, fog, all provide new visual transformations and a stimulus to discussion and other forms of creative work apart from visual art.

In all that has been mentioned the child is being led to explore new visual experience which moves away from what he has been accustomed to drawing and painting, away from the stereotyped subject matter based on so-called imagination. He is required to find new ways of expressing what he wants to say. Imagination is not the escape from reality but the transformation of experience into new forms.

Another way to keep children's interest and confidence alive as they move into the difficult period when they tend to reject their own work, is by the introduction of media which offer little possibility of creating naturalistic work. Lino-cuts, mosaic, junk-modelling and constructions of various sorts, collage, embroidery, tapestry are all examples of media which have their own distinctive characteristics which encourage a decorative or abstract manner of working, without this being imposed arbitrarily on the child. Materials which make technical demands calling for special skills and forethought challenge the child and engage his interest and respect. It is in this way that some children can be encouraged to continue creative work.

The two approaches outlined are not mutually exclusive. The purpose of drawing may be to provide starting points for, say, lino-cutting or mosaic, and a child is often more willing to draw if the idea is put to him that he is collecting information and notes rather than making a picture. A sheet of drawings which are crowded together, some one way up and some another, each an attempt to discover and record some new facet of the object under observation, is a better product than a 'picture' in which the child may have struggled with problems of space and proportion with little success or satisfaction. Children can be encouraged in this way of thinking if they are shown reproductions of pages of artists' note-books – Michelangelo and Leonardo da Vinci offer particularly good examples.

Art and the adolescent
However good the teaching, not all children will continue to find satisfaction in the active pursuit of the visual arts as they move through adolescence. Some will find that other forms of expressive work suit them better. In this case, it is likely that there will be many points of contact, and the sensitivity developed in one art often predisposes the child to be sympathetic towards and interested in other forms. Others may for various reasons reject all arts, and although this issue lies outside the age range considered here, undoubtedly the teaching which leads up to the period of adolescence is a major factor in determining pupils' attitudes to the arts. It is important that no attempt is made to preserve 'child art', and pupils must be given every help to adjust towards a more adult concept of art. It must be recognised that many pupils are not going to be able to draw and paint in the 'realistic' way which they think is the style they should emulate, and for these it is helpful if activities are offered which are not image based. Textile printing, weaving, pottery, metal work, jewellery, etc, involve consideration of colour and form and require the pupil to make creative decisions in a way which is comparable to drawing and painting or any of the other 'art' activities. Images can, of course, be brought into these crafts, but they are not an essential part and the pupil can avoid them if he wants to.

Materials
The discussion so far has been concerned with children's imagery and sources of ideas, but all art brings together two basic concerns, image and material. Of the latter little has

8 *Tree* by an eleven year old girl

provide visual stimulus, for growth in one aspect is dependant on growth in the other. An urgent need to find a way of expressing something will push a child into new ways of using material; exploration of material will provide new ways of expression. Figure 8 was made by a girl of eleven. She began by messing about with liquid paint and inks with no particular idea in mind. Suddenly the way the colour had run and the textures created suggested to her that what was on her paper could be made into a tree.

Curiosity about the nature of materials is manifest at a very early age, and the way in which babies will explore their food by squashing and squeezing it has already been mentioned. When children first enter the reception class they bring with them widely differing experiences. Some will have had ample opportunity to play with paint and clay, sand and water; others, for various reasons, will have been deprived of this. This difference in background is clearly shown in the way the children approach the opportunities offered by the school; some will want merely to play around with paint whilst others go straight into the activity of painting pictures. The teacher has to provide as wide a range of materials as she can, and encourage their free use. At this stage there is little need for more than this, although a discreet suggestion may send a child on a profitable line of exploration. It may, for example, be valuable to give a little simple instruction on how to make a print with a potato or from a leaf, or to collect some tools and objects with which children can explore the making of marks in clay. Children learn much from watching each other, and sometimes the teacher may find that the success of one child has led to many others imitating him. This is not necessarily a bad thing for it usually only involves some simple process which the children can use later for their own more personal ends.

been said. It has been mentioned that a child discovers that his scribbling can be given meaning, and from this point onward his development is as much dependant on his continued exploration of materials as it is on external experience stimulating him to evolve more elaborate images. The teacher must therefore be equally concerned to provide opportunity to explore and control materials as he is to

Structuring experience

As children move through the primary school there is value in the teacher structuring exploratory experiences with specific types of material. Drawing is fundamentally a matter of making marks on a surface. There are many tools which will make marks apart from those which are particularly designed for the job. Each tool, whether it be

9 A drawing in charcoal by a nine year old girl

improvised or not, has its own range and quality of mark. One task can be to take a tool and explore its range – how thick a mark, how thin, how delicate, how bold. Figure 9 shows a nine year old girl's use of charcoal which varies from a very fine, delicate mark to a thick, bold one. This capacity in a child to use a tool or material through the full range of its possibilities is one of the indications of sensitive art teaching, and one of the criteria a teacher should apply in the evaluation of his teaching. Children can be encouraged to try out many unusual tools for drawing, for instance an old scrubbing brush or a tooth brush. All sorts of objects – sticks, twigs, feathers, paper spills, straws, rags, rope, string, blocks of wood, bones, fingers – can be used with black paint or ink to produce unpredictable effects.

Each child will produce different results and find some tools more satisfying than others, for each child has his own particular approach to using tools. A mark is a record of how a particular tool has contacted the paper. It is, in a sense, the record of a gesture and therefore expressive of the mood and personality of the person making the mark. Some children attack their paper boldly, aggressively, whilst others come with a delicate controlled movement; each will find a type of tool best suited to his needs.

Not all marks need be drawn. In the section on printing there is a description of how objects can be used to give printed or stamped marks and this is a valuable extension of exploratory mark-making. It is valuable too, to see what happens when marks are repeated at close intervals, for this leads a child into pattern and texture making.

There is little point in undertaking this kind of exploration unless it is related to observation. Children have little use for purposeless exercises, but such work can lead into the study of markings on birds or fish, or looking at the patterns created by stacked wood, bottles or bricks, or careful observation of the hearts of flowers.

Exploration must be a continuous process, and as children get older they are capable of sustained investigation into what a particular tool can achieve. This is an opening into the study of how artists exploit the means at their disposal to achieve special effects. Artists such as John Piper or Henry Moore (Shelter Drawings) would be especially rewarding if approached from this point of view.

Painting

Drawing and painting have not been considered separately so far because the concern has been with the way children's imagery develops and with the influences which affect it. In many cases children are still drawing when they are using paint. This is especially true of young children who draw with a brush and then fill in the outlines – often with a completely different colour. There is, however, a developmental process in painting which tends to go parallel with what has been discussed in terms of drawing. Just as children begin drawing by scribbling, so they often begin painting by stroking, smearing and scrubbing paint across a surface. Much depends on what sort of paint a child is offered. If he is faced with pots of ready mixed liquid colour with a brush in each, he will more than likely make a linear drawing in colour. If faced with a set of powder colour or tempera blocks, or even the old-fashioned painting box which in various forms still exists, the young child of three or four is likely to spend a happy time mixing colour without transferring any to paper. Later, the paint will be put on the paper in patches of colour with no attempt to depict objects or any drawing of lines. Such painting is a spontaneous activity in which much of the pleasure comes from the mixing of the colour rather than applying it to the paper, and this sensuous delight in the paint itself is important for the development of painting later on.

Children alternate between this 'area' approach and the linear one they use with their drawing. A child will, for example, draw 'Daddy' with a brush and then fill in the shapes created with different colours. Later on the brush drawing may be replaced by a charcoal or pencil drawing which is then lost in the subsequent filling-in with paint. This is a regrettable step and alien to a child's proper development in painting. Very often one sees beautiful drawings which are virtually destroyed by the over-painting. Children realise this, and many are reluctant to begin painting when they have spent time and trouble in developing a drawing. If they can be encouraged from the beginning to paint without preliminary drawing in charcoal or crayon they are more likely to 'think' in areas of colour and to enjoy colour for its own sake. Commonly, though, a teacher is given a class which has acquired poor habits or lost confidence as a result of previous teaching and the teacher is faced with a situation which requires remedial action. Such children may understandably resent being asked to paint directly without preliminary drawing. An intermediate step is to ask them to draw with white chalk on white paper, or with some neutral colour if their paper is grey or buff. The advantage of this is that the drawing is difficult to see and they are not tempted to commit themselves to a finished drawing and, in addition, the drawing itself tends to disappear without trace as the painting progresses. When charcoal or pencil is used it often shows through the paint in an obtrusive way.

Explorations

As with drawing materials, there is need for opportunity to explore painting media and tools in a structured way. Each child needs to discover what for him is the appropriate way of using various types of paint, and there is no one right way that all children should use. There is still the idea that children should use big brushes and work at easels, and that their art should look 'free'. Children vary, however; some are happiest and freest working on a small scale in a delicate controlled manner; others find that their right scale and style demand large paper and big brushes. It is important that children should have the freedom to choose which is appropriate for them and the task they are about to tackle. This does not mean that the teacher should never restrict the children to a particular scale. The child who always works on a small scale may never have had the encouragement or the opportunity to do anything else, and he is in need of wider experience in order that he may choose from knowledge rather than habit. Similarly children who have always worked on a large scale may benefit from the challenge of small scale, controlled work. This is a matter for the professional judgment of the teacher, who may apply a constraint for educational reasons based on his assessment of the children's needs.

There are many sorts of paints and many ways in which paints can be used, and there is value in investigating what tools can be improvised, as there is with drawing. Paint can be dribbled, poured, dusted-on, spotted onto dry paper, on to wet paper and on to paint that is already there. Paint can be dropped on to wet paper and the paper lifted and tilted. Thin paint can be brushed over a wax drawing or rubbing. There are many such activities which encourage children to think about the materials they are using and to gain a better understanding of their potential. Many of the effects they produce will be accidental, but this does not matter. After a while they will be able to control the sort of accident which will happen and to gauge with increasing accuracy the result that will emerge. As a by-product of this play with paint, children become sensitive to qualities of colour and texture in a way which is not possible if paint is only used in a controlled manner. This sensitivity is a basis for developing a child's responsiveness to the natural world. The markings on a pebble or in a slab of marble are not unlike the effects that can be obtained by letting liquid paints run and merge together and the enjoyment of one is heightened by experience of the other. 'Marbling' is itself an activity in which children find great delight.

Experimental sessions with paint in isolation from other experiences are of limited value. Their virtue lies in their being part of a curriculum designed to extend the child's awareness and sensitivity. It is vital to assess the learning which takes place through a particular activity rather than be over-concerned with the end product on paper. All the initial exploratory experiences that have been discussed can be developed and refined and the child made increasingly sensitive to new qualities and possibilities.

Colour

The development of a personal sense of colour is considered later and it is only necessary here to point out that, as with drawing, there is increasing need as a child becomes older to relate painting to objective study, both inside and outside the classroom. Children in the upper classes of the primary school are capable of making careful colour studies in paint from objects such as leaves, shells, flowers and anything which can arouse their interest. Where weather and local conditions permit, there is every advantage in working out-of-doors in a similar way.

Imagination

Enough has been said already to establish the importance of using the child's environment as a source of imagery. Without this a child's imagination can only be supplied with images from second-hand sources. But this should not limit the child to a purely observation approach to painting and drawing. Unless he has the opportunity and the encouragement to use his imagination upon the observed data there is a danger that he will produce careful, rather cold studies which may lack any personal quality. Therefore the importance of an imaginative approach to materials must also be stressed, for this is the basis for a richer response to experience.

The value of drawing and painting

Making images or pictures provides a child with an opportunity to explore the inner world of himself and the outer world of his family, his school, and the wider environment with which he becomes increasingly involved as he grows through the primary school. This exploration is intuitive and the child, by the nature of the activity, is not required to put into words what he is doing, but in his choice of subject, in his choice of tools and materials and in the way in which he develops his work, he is sorting out his emotions and ideas and relating himself to them. Through this activity he is able to get a better grasp of his experience, to understand and assimilate it because he has given it order in his terms. To give a concrete illustration; a child who has visited the local fire station and returns to the classroom to paint a picture of the firemen going to a fire is

a   ordering and using in an active way factual information gained about uniform, equipment and so on

b   developing ideas and emotions about the urgency of the situation and, intuitively, finding ways of expressing this sense of urgency by pictorial means.

In this process he will experience in a vicarious way, within the limitations of his age and development, something of the fireman's feelings and thoughts, and capture something of the excitement of the moment. As a result of his painting such a picture he is provided with opportunities to discuss his ideas with his class mates and the teacher, and further development through elaboration, or correction of erroneous ideas, can occur. His painting, if he is a primary school child will almost certainly be schematic, but it may contain a great amount of factual information which is evidence of his concern with the subject matter, and no attempt to 'correct' the painting should be made.

Painting, however, is not only concerned with images but with the materials used, and every painting should add something to the child's knowledge of colour and his way of using it so that he is better able to tackle succeeding pictures. The shapes and colours of the things he sees and touches are better as the source of his inspiration than the whimsical fantasy which one finds so often in children's work. This is not to deny any place for imagination or fantasy but even the wildest monster or most hideous witch may be derived from the study of actuality. The use of magnifying glasses or microscopes on insect or other minute life forms may reveal a horrific world. Playing with lighting and various props can create the basis for 'witch' pictures. It is, however, with the world of people and things that the teacher should be primarily concerned and it is a sensitive, affectionate response to this world that the teacher should be aiming for.

Summary

Drawing and painting offer ways of learning about the world and relating to it. The teacher's role is to focus the child's attention on various aspects, and by discussion help the child to structure his experience so that it becomes manageable and he can express it adequately. Experience of the materials of painting and drawing is an essential component of growth in creative work and the teacher should provide a wide range of materials and stimuli which provoke its use in an imaginative way. Towards the upper end of the age range this means that the teacher himself needs to be able to see possibilities in the school and its surroundings, and also in the world of ideas of which the pupils are increasingly aware. Children can be moved for example by the plight of refugees and the sick and old, and not all art work need be a direct response to things local to the school. The danger is that children will merely reproduce memories of pictures they have seen and the teacher's role here is to help the children to clothe their ideas in forms derived from their own experience. Given that the children have had a rich experience both of working from visual stimuli and of materials, they are likely to be able to deal successfully with themes which make special demands on their imagination. Most religious painting is of this category – imaginative painting based on an intimate knowledge of the visual world.

10 *A man with a dumper truck* by a four year old boy

11   A drawing by a five year old boy. Top: *The artist* complete with painting knife and easel drawn in the artist's studio. Bottom: Drawn immediately on returning from a walk with the family

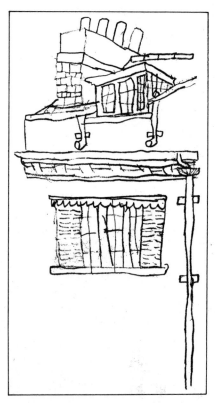

12   A drawing by a nine year old child after a walk around the streets near his school

13 Work resulting from an experimental mark making session

14   *My family* by a four year old boy

15   Drawing by a twelve year old girl

16   Reference to visual
material lays the foundation for
work in a variety of crafts

17 Painted curtain by six year old children

18 *My cat* by a six year old girl

PHOTOGRAPHY

Recording

Although drawing and colour studies, possibly augmented by written notes, will always be the main methods of recording the visual environment, the camera is becoming increasingly valuable. With younger children the camera can be used by the teacher to record visits and other events, and slides can then be used to stimulate discussion and refresh the children's memories of important aspects of whatever was seen. Children at the top of the primary school can use the camera themselves.

The camera

The importance of the camera at this stage lies in its capacity to heighten perception. There is little value in taking photographs of everyday scenes for they are not likely to reveal anything new. It is better to use the camera to record the less obvious and to concentrate on particular aspects of a topic. For example, if the theme 'pattern' were taken, visits to building sites could provide photographs of patterns made by stacks of bricks, tiles, drain-pipes and the like. Timber stacks are also interesting if viewed end-on. The patterns made unconsciously by men stacking units in a rhythmic process might be compared with the more random patterns made by bricks when they have been tipped from a lorry into a pile. 'Texture' might be another theme, and one could look for textures in tree trunks, paving stones, roofs and walls, on beaches, on cliffs or in quarries – the possibilities are numerous. Implicit in these suggestions is the need to get close to the subject matter and to isolate the central interest from the surroundings. It is this that the viewfinder of the camera can help children to do. If it is impossible to get a camera, little viewfinders made from cardboard will help children to see the value of concentrating on essentials. Old slide mounts are excellent for this purpose, but it is not difficult to make similar ones from thin card.

Photographic equipment and materials

Cheap cameras can provide good results, but if it is possible to obtain a single-lens reflex camera, this is admirable. These cameras open up new possibilities of getting close to minute subjects and photographing them life-size or larger. This can be done by inserting extension tubes between the lens and the camera body; with these it is possible to photograph, for example, the centre of a flower or section of a cabbage from close up (see figure 20). The second great advantage of the single-lens reflex camera is that what is seen in the view-finder is what is actually photographed. With the cheaper, view-finder camera, the view-finder does not see exactly the same view as the lens, and this can be a drawback when doing close-up work. Single-lens reflex cameras can be obtained cheaply second hand, and any teacher interested in this approach should contact the Local Education Authority Adviser who is responsible for audio-visual aids. Alternatively, any reputable photographic shop would be able to give advice, and through good local contacts of this nature cheaper film might be obtainable. Often out-dated stock can be bought at reduced prices and for most purposes it is perfectly adequate. For black and white work, film can be bought in bulk for loading into 35 mm cassettes, and this makes it possible to reduce costs very considerably. The film loading must be done in total darkness, but a properly equipped darkroom is not essential for this. Often a room facing away from street lighting can be used for this purpose at night. Darkrooms for processing the film are not difficult to improvise, and this is being done in many junior schools. It is not the intention to go deeply into photographic processes in this book because there are many suitable textbooks available, but it should be emphasised that processing films and making prints from them is not difficult and need not be excessively expensive.

An alternative to making enlargements is to make black and white transparencies from black and white negatives.

This is the least expensive and simplest process, since the original film can be developed by photographic shops quite cheaply and cuts out the need for any work in complete darkness. To make such slides any stockroom without a window will make an adequate darkroom. The results are by no means perfect; the slides may well be grainy and blemished. Nevertheless they introduce children to photographic processes and they provide a record which can be projected for the whole class to see and discuss. Detailed instructions are given at the end of the book.

Projectors and slide-making

The teacher's main concern is with the learning that takes place as a result of a particular activity, rather than with the end product, although it may be an important indication of what learning has taken place. From this point of view it is not necessary for every lesson to result in some product such as a drawing or a painting. The teacher may provide a certain type of experience without demanding that it be recorded in some particular way. The objective may be to encourage curiosity, experimental attitudes and increased sensitivity to form and colour.

Working with slide projectors offers scope for this sort of activity. 35 mm slide mounts, which consist of two thin sheets of glass in plastic interlocking frames, can be bought. Normally a colour slide is sandwiched between the glasses, but any small, very thin materials may be substituted. These frames, however, are quite expensive and can present problems for young children, since the glass is easily broken and the slide is rather difficult to assemble. A cheaper and easier alternative is to buy or improvise card mounts and use any transparent adhesive material such as *Fablon*, *Tacky-back* or even wide *Sellotape* to bridge the opening in the mount. The easiest technique is to take a card mount, or a mount-sized piece of card with a 'window' cut in it, and stick a piece of transparent adhesive material across it. The slide is then turned over and the material to be mounted, a leaf skeleton for instance, is placed down on the adhesive surface. A second piece of the adhesive material is placed on top so that the specimen is sandwiched in place. For first attempts, pocket fluff, human hair, small feathers, fibres, onion skins, flower petals, small seeds, dandelion fluff, etc could be used. When these slides are projected, the effect is astonishing and often very beautiful. Colour is lost unless the substances are particularly thin and transparent and what is projected on the screen is really a shadow, but this is not a great disadvantage.

A development of this work is to use coloured transparent materials – cellophanes especially – to make up slides. By overlapping them, children can explore the effects of mixing light (see chapter on colour, page 36). Interesting effects can also be made by putting liquid paint or inks with a small spot of oil between the glass or plastic. Usually there is sufficient space to allow the oil and paint to flow around, and both gravity and the heat from the lamp will produce movement in this image. The most strange and exciting shapes can be produced in this way. It is best not to overload the slide, and if small dusty particles can be included, the movement becomes particularly obvious. Crushed charcoal or lead pencil sharpenings are suitable for this purpose.

This is a fascinating process and once children have begun to realise the possibilities they become very involved and inventive in what they try out. There are many variations, and if two projectors are available so that two images can be projected on to the one screen, a new range of possibilities is opened up. Improvised slides in one projector could be combined with photographic slides in the other. By holding a piece of card in front of the lens the image can be blocked off from the screen, and this can be done rhythmically to music, so that the screen has the image flashing off and on in time to the music. With two projectors in use, and the possibility of changing slides as well, the work can become very complex but well worth exploring with secondary school children. Teachers who are interested in working with drama and movement will see possibilities of using a combined approach. Slides projected very large onto walls create an environment in which drama or dance can take place, and the movement itself can be enhanced by moving through the images.

The imaginative models mentioned earlier can also be illuminated by slides projected onto them or on to the background. The model of the train crossing the bridge could have had a landscape slide projected behind it. Slides of sky and the sea have obvious applications.

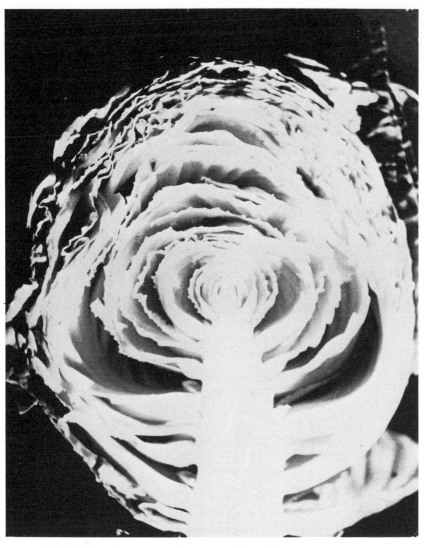

19–21   Using the camera to get close up to the subject matter

COLOUR

Colour is an important element in our lives. We all have our likes and dislikes about colour, and most people can make their choices with confidence when it is a simple issue of what colour to have for a single article such as a ball-point pen, a diary or a car. When the issue is choosing one colour to go with another many people are less confident; they tend to play safe and accept simple rules – grey and pink look well together, orange and pink do not. Fashion plays an important part in many choices and over different periods particular ranges of colour become dominant, and many people are guided in their decisions by what is currently popular. The teacher's task is to encourage the development of a personal sense of colour in the pupils so that they are open to a wider range of possibilities and can make choices within the general trend of the times with greater discrimination and confidence. There are various ways by which the teacher can achieve this objective.

Providing experiences

Children must have opportunities to enjoy colour for its own sake, to explore coloured materials and paints, and to discuss colour and the interaction of one with another. In brief they must have experience of colour separated from the business of making pictures. Colour in painting is obviously very important, and any development of colour sensitivity in other activities will enhance its use in children's pictorial work. It is doubtful, however, if painting alone provides enough opportunity for such sensitivity to develop.

The young child shows a marked preference for positive bright colours. When he reaches the stage of filling in the linear paintings he has made, his choice will be based on emotional responses; he often chooses colours because he likes them rather than because they are descriptive of a sky, a house or a tree. The subtle colour usage of the adult artist in which colours are chosen because they harmonise or interact with each other may be deliberate and supported by knowledge and experience, but the young child's usage is intuitive and based on his immediate response to colour. While some children do seem to possess an inherent colour sense, and put them together in a very personal way, teachers cannot assume that, left to their own devices, the children will develop anything more than a very simple response to colour. Looking at paintings produced by fifth and sixth form pupils in secondary schools, it is apparent that for many the understanding of colour is still at a rudimentary stage, and that they have developed surprisingly little since early junior school. The teacher should devise a sequential programme of experiences in which the child explores colour, develops conceptual understanding of it and uses it in creative work.

Developing sensitivity

Many children who enter infant schools have had little encouragement to discuss colour. Indeed many reception class children cannot name all the common colours. It is therefore important for the teacher to provide situations in which colours are identified, named, and discussed. Perhaps the most obvious approach is through the collection and display of objects within a given colour range. 'Interest tables' can sometimes be devoted to such a theme and it would be possible for different groups of children to concentrate on a particular colour – yellows for one, blues for another and so on. With older children towards the top of the infant school the teacher might want to make this a more subtle exercise and perhaps whites might be taken, or browns would be another rich field to explore. Various ideas can be explored thus. Clearly there is visual evidence that there is not one blue but thousands, and discussion can focus on how they differ. The concepts of lighter and darker, and green/blue and red/blue, for example, can be built up. Discussion can range over qualities of surface – shiny blues, dull blues. Blues can be named and associations can be explored – sky-blue, ice-blue, navy-blue, air-force blue – and personal preferences can be brought out. Each colour can be treated in a similar way and the teacher can build up a valuable vocabulary of colour words.

What has been suggested here as suitable for young children is equally applicable to older children, if their previous experience has been limited. Naturally the actual approach to the children would be modified to suit their ages, and greater subtlety and discrimination might be expected. One could move more quickly into an examination of greys for instance, and relate this to observation of walls and buildings within the immediate environs of the school. With older primary school or secondary school children, ideas about colour could be consciously applied in picture making. The teacher could discuss moods suggested by particular colours – sombre, cold, sad, bright, gay, aggressive, quiet – and perhaps relate this to comparable effects obtained by particular sounds and instruments in music, or the effects achieved in poetry by the rhythms and sounds. The children might then like to explore the particular ranges of colour suited to the subject they are painting. This approach to colour may lead into imaginative work which takes the children beyond their immediate experience, but it can also be rooted in study of the changing visual world around them. For instance, they can see what happens to colour under moonlight or at sunset. They can be asked to make collections of natural objects. From these they can learn various things – whether the colours are muted or positive; how many different greens or greys there are, how the surface quality of the object affects the intensity of the colour. At some levels of ability or age range this will be an opportunity for discussion in which the teacher draws the children on to make finer and finer distinctions and leads them into giving their personal reaction to colours. In this way both their ability to discriminate between colours and their responses to them are developed and heightened. With other groups of different ages and abilities such an approach could be based on written responses, although there is a danger that too much insistence on written answers can dim the responsiveness of the children, and the teacher loses the opportunity for spontaneous interaction with the children which the discussion situation provides. Obviously the discussions of colour in this way lead directly into objective studies using paint or other appropriate media.

A slightly different approach is to take a natural object, say, a flower, and to use the colours found in it as the basis for a painting or other work – designs in fabric or a piece of weaving, for example. If children are capable of appreciating proportions, then stripes in a piece of weaving could be based on the proportions of colour in the flower. There are many ways of dealing with this. With a blue anemone the child could estimate the relative areas of blue, black-indigo and white; he could put a ruler across the flower and measure the bands of colour and take the proportions from such linear data; he could use the data to work out the areas of colour and use these proportions; or he could arrive at the areas by drawing round the flower on squared paper, drawing in the other areas by judgment and then counting squares of each colour to arrive at the correct proportions. The fundamental objective of such an exercise is to develop some appreciation of the way colour effects are dependant on the proportions of colour in any arrangement.

Colour games
Such exercises are of limited value, and many children will need an approach based more on games. Marion Richardson, one of the great pioneers in art education, devised colour matching games using skeins of wool, and this principle can be used to devise games of various forms. A child, having been shown a particular colour, has then to select from a range of colours the one which matches. In Marion Richardson's version the children had to remember the colour they had been shown and select it from a collection at the other end of the room. This is a sophisticated version suitable for older children but infant and junior children would need to work in a more immediate situation first. Many card games can be adapted to this purpose: Colour Snap is one possibility, in which cards coloured on one side are used. Simple colours can be given at first and

22 Revolving colour disc

then the pack made increasingly subtle as the children become used to the game, until it is being played with ranges of greys, greens, browns. There is another simple game sometimes called Memory or Pelmanism in which a pack of cards is spread face down and the children take turns in turning the cards over to find 'pairs'. This can be played with a pack of cards similar to the snap cards. Dominoes is yet another game that can be converted from numbers to colours.

The use of such games is not a substitute for art work but an adjunct to it. They can be reserved for odd times such as wet break times, or can be adapted for some special teaching linked to some particular objective, or reserved for groups of children who present special difficulties. Unlike most of the activities which go on under the umbrella of art they are capable of incorporating highly specific learning, and therefore worth considering as part of the resources at the command of the teacher.

Colour and light
The slide projector is another source of colour experience. 35 mm slide mounts, either the glass and plastic sort, or cardboard mounts as mentioned in the earlier section, can be used to make experimental slides using coloured cellophanes, off-cuts of 'gels' from stage lighting, translucent flower petals, transparent inks and the like. When these slides are projected the result is often unexpected and exciting. It is possible to use paints and inks and oil in all sorts of combinations, and the repellent reaction of oil and water will often provide moving patterns of strange and complex character which fascinate and delight children.

Projectors can also be used as sources of illumination. Using slides of a single colour, objects or pictures or people can be illuminated with different colours, and the strange effects noted. For example, a child wearing a yellow sweater can be illuminated by a red slide and then by a blue one. If two projectors are available even more exciting results can be obtained. Red and blue projected together from two projectors produce brilliant 'shadows' from objects placed in the beams, and since there are two beams of light the shadows are doubled and each of a different colour. Any pair of colours will produce a similar effect and can lead into discussion of the differences between mixing pigments and mixing light.

Colour science
There is, of course, a clear lead into looking at light and colour from a scientific point of view, and many worthwhile experiments can be set up which will increase children's experience and knowledge of colour. Experiments can be carried out with colour wheels. These are simply discs of card, or paper stuck on card, which are revolved at various speeds. Different colour effects will be obtained according to how they have been painted. Newton discs made from the primary colours should, in theory, appear white when revolved, but in practice seldom do. It is probably better to concentrate on a more experimental approach in which patterns of stripes and dots are painted on the discs and revolved to see what happens. Revolving the discs can be done in a number of simple ways. A pencil or cocktail stick inserted through the centre of a disc will

turn it into a top. Alternatively, two holes can be made and a loop of string threaded through as in the traditional children's whizzer, see figure 22. Discs can be revolved on a record player using 78 rpm, or placed on the sanding disc of an electric drill and revolved at very high speeds. Pottery wheels, banding wheels or cake turntables can also be used. Many boys would be interested in making a device out of Meccano to serve this purpose; this would at the same time involve them in a piece of functional creative thinking.

Investigations of the physical properties of light is another field of interest for some teachers and pupils. It is possible to let a shaft of sunlight shine through a hole in a sheet of black paper and through a prism onto white paper. This will show the white light broken up into the colours of the spectrum, and the names and order of the colours in the spectrum can be noted. A slide projector and a prism can give comparable effects. The question of where else spectrums are found can be raised. Children will not be long in volunteering 'the rainbow' but there are other sources too. Oil slicks on wet roads give just such an effect and some children rather poetically refer to them as 'dead rainbows'. Bubbles are yet another source of the same spectrum effect. A clear sky at sunset also gives the spectrum colours in their right order from red at the horizon through the oranges, yellows and so on to indigo in the east.

Consideration of the spectrum of normal white light can lead directly into consideration of other sources of light which give strange effects. Why does fluorescent lighting alter the appearance of certain colours? How does the street lighting affect the way things look? The depth to which such topics can be pursued depends on many factors, but particularly the teacher's own knowledge and enthusiasm and the age and ability of the children. With young children there would be value in observing the changes of colour effected by different lighting, even if the pupils were not capable of going any deeper into the topic. At this observational level colour experience can be provided by the burning of certain salts in a bunsen burner flame. Sodium chloride will give yellow; barium chloride, apple green; copper, blue/green; strontium, red; potassium, violet. Objects or pieces of coloured felt placed close to the flame will change radically in colour appearance. The room must be dark for the full effect to be obtained.

23 Studying the coloured reflections that can be seen when blowing a plastic bubble

Camouflage and display
The importance of referring to the environment for visual information has already been stressed, but one can also look at colour in nature from its functional point of view. For example, one can see how it serves to make an animal merge into its surroundings (camouflage), or to stand out from them (display). Whilst colour is important in this consideration, it soon becomes clear that pattern and shape play a major role too. There is a practical approach to this topic – objects (perhaps model cars, tanks, aeroplanes, would be particularly suitable for boys to work with) could be painted so that they blended with a particular background. In one recent piece of work in which a small group of children were working with students, the students prepared a number of milk bottles painted bright colours which were placed against various painted backgrounds. The children's task was to paint the bottles so that they 'disappeared'. This they achieved with considerable success,

although it is true that they had only considered each bottle in a particular place and their combinations of colours and pattern were related to a particular piece of background. The exercise could have been developed by requiring the bottle to be placed anywhere against a background and still blend with the surroundings.

This and similar exercises can be reversed, with the objective being to make an object stand out from its surroundings, and it is important that children should encounter both sets of problems. What lies behind these is an important group of concepts concerned with colour, tone, pattern and form. For example, the concept of contrast is central to both display and camouflage; in the former it is maximised, in the latter reduced to a minimum. Contrast may involve both colour and tone, and the separation of these two concepts is again an important one, although most children would not take the concept of tone much beyond the simple idea of lighter and darker until they were of secondary school age. Consideration of pattern involves consideration of the scale of the pattern in the background as opposed to that of the object. A simple form seen against a richly broken background will stand out very clearly, even if colour and tone are not markedly different. It becomes necessary to introduce pattern of the same scale and same

nature on to the object. This requires attention being given to the nature of the shapes of the pattern, whether they are mostly vertical, jagged or soft, mostly uniform or much varied. The extent to which such considerations are verbalised and discussed between teacher and pupils and amongst the pupils themselves will vary enormously, but however simply the task is treated the children are put in a position in which they are required to pay careful attention to all the aspects listed and drawn into making finer and finer distinctions.

Relating to other work

There is little point in doing this kind of activity unless the learning is related to other work, and this is why it is important that some attempt should be made to clarify the concepts underlying the activities. Fabric printing, weaving, embroidery, interior design, ceramics, dress-design, to give just a few examples, are areas in which awareness of the basic concept is valuable, and in any area of art activity, however subjective and personal, the vocabulary arising from the colour work outlined provides the basis for a more meaningful discussion than is often possible at present.

LOOKING AT PAINTING AND SCULPTURE

Art education, as well as developing children's expressive urge to communicate feelings and thoughts and extending their powers of observation, should also help them develop a sense of discrimination and visual awareness. Making art objects involves children in decision making of a kind which demands understanding and evaluation, but if they are to develop an understanding of visual communication in all its varied forms, making art objects alone is not enough.

One important area of investigation is the study of the great art of the past, and in particular the art of the twentieth century which often has more relevance to children's work.

Unless art education in schools does something to introduce children to the painting and sculptures which are part of our cultural heritage, it has failed in one of its most important tasks. This does not necessarily involve more art history and appreciation. In fact it is doubtful if children in the age range with which we are concerned would profit from any formal course. What is wanted is a lively, enquiring response to the art of the past and present and an understanding that artists have dealt with the same sort of problems with which the children are concerned.

The most direct approach to 'Art' for children is through their own work. For example, they may have been studying faces – perhaps making careful studies of eyes, using their partners or working from small mirrors, looking carefully at the colours in faces, watching how the muscles create the various expressions, looking at the overall shapes, talking about the characters to be seen on the bus or at the shops, making drawings and paintings which are based on these starting points. These children are likely to enjoy an introduction to Breugel, to the paintings of the Italian Renaissance, to Dutch portrait painting, to Renoir, Modigliani, Peter Blake – the list is endless.

Or to take a different case: the boy who has been exploring a piece of wood or stone through carving may be in just the right receptive state to appreciate the sculpture of Barbara Hepworth; or, if he has been concerned with some image, perhaps his attention should be turned to primitive carvings or Chinese jade. A group of children who have produced a large frieze might appreciate Egyptian or Assyrian friezes. As they approach the end of the primary schools, almost any work done by children offers an opportunity to introduce them to some aspect of the art of the past or the present. This contact with great art will show them many styles which are very different from the photographic realism which is the commonly held lay concept of what art should aim for, and it will help to give them confidence in their own personal vision. As children grow older and move into the early teens it is important that they understand the process of art as a process of selection and communication of what is personally significant to the artist, and not as a process of reproduction or imitation. The defeat of the young adolescent as far as art is concerned is not necessarily rooted in his own incompetence but in his inability to match his personal imagery with what he thinks art is about. His concept of art has failed to develop because the emphasis has been on *doing* at the expense of understanding and relating the art of the classroom to the art of the past and present.

There are many opportunities to do this. Books, slides, reproductions and films can provide many examples. The BBC, with Radio Vision (which consists of colour film strips linked to radio broadcasts) and various television programmes, provides an excellent service.

Children should be presented with a range of examples and styles. They can be encouraged to look at the way, for example, Goya, Manet, Paul Nash and Picasso responded to war, or how Rembrandt or Dali depicted the crucifixion.

There are many books on individual artists or groups of artists now available, many of them very inexpensive, and all schools could have a selection in their libraries. Some schools have reproductions on their walls, and an increasing number of local authorities are operating a free loan service of reproductions and original works.

Many public galleries offer educational services which include talks, guided tours and sometimes questionnaires about the exhibits. It can be useful for the teacher to visit the gallery beforehand, provide an introduction, duplicate lists of questions and follow up with a discussion. The great historic homes are also sources of much great art.

Children can be encouraged to choose a work of art to write about. Often pictures provide excellent stimulus for creative writing. The following poem was written by an eleven year old girl after looking at the *White Dogs* by Thomas Gainsborough.

Two pairs of bright glassy eyes
Appeared from a dark gloomy hole,
Emerging slowly and carefully,
Trembling with fear.
Beautiful dogs with long thick fur,
Had hidden there all day long,
Not daring to move
In case they were found.
For their master was cruel and wicked,
They had no food, nor any drink,
Now for the first time that day
They breathed cool fresh air,
Then the feeling of satisfaction
Crept through their bodies,
As if warm fire was turned on,
They felt free,
Free to do as they chose.

Most areas of the country have their own craftsmen – sculptors, potters, wrought iron workers. Many of them are willing to show groups of children how they practise their craft in their studios, or they may bring examples of their work to the school.

Two- and three-dimensional works of art offer many sources of ideas and investigation for children: the social behaviour of the people can be seen – styles of dress, methods of travel and living conditions are recorded. Portraits give a visual record of famous people – the Royal Family, politicians, writers, musicians, actors, generals and admirals, as well as those with less claim to fame. Stories of artists, such as Van Gogh or Gaughin, provide insight into the nature of creative work.

Study of paintings leads to a new awareness of colour, shape, design and imagery, and acquaintance with sculpture, mosaic, tapestry, stained glass, and other crafts helps in understanding construction, casting, and methods of creative productions.

Most public galleries will have exhibits concerned in some way with the local area, and many galleries, while covering a range of periods, styles and subject matter, tend to be particularly strong in one area. Birmingham Art Gallery is noted for its collection of works by the Pre-Raphaelite Brotherhood and Norwich Museum for paintings by the Norwich School of Landscape Painters. A teacher, having decided on a particular area of study, may approach the curator of a museum and ask for help and advice concerning relevant visual material. Reference should also be made to the catalogue of exhibits.

Scrutiny of the art books in the public library is also an enjoyable way to learn something of the tremendous potential offered by the whole field of art history.

One might begin in a different way, with an interest in a particular period – England in the eighteenth century for example. A study of the works of William Hogarth, Thomas Gainsborough, Joshua Reynolds, George Stubbs, George Morland, Joseph Wright of Derby, and Thomas Rowlandson, provides an astonishing wealth of visual material, illustrating many aspects of urban and rural social life in that century.

Reference to general books such as *A Concise History of English Painting* by William Gaunt provides general background information, and together with the bibliography, provide a basis for more detailed study.

COLLAGE

Materials

Collage, the fixing of objects to a surface to form a composition, is included in many art classes. Virtually any material, natural or man-made, may be used, and collage-making draws on the intuitive response to the qualities of shape, colour and texture that the materials possess. Because of the range of materials, it offers tremendous scope for picture making of any scale, from small individual efforts to large group projects. Much of the material is found or can be bought very cheaply.

In many art classes the materials are restricted to cuttings from colour supplements, pieces of fabric and patterns from wallpaper books. If the teacher is to use a wide range of materials, the difficulties of the collection and storage of materials present themselves – but neither of these problems is insurmountable. Collecting the material needs to be a joint enterprise on the part of teachers, parents and children. Many teachers build contacts with local shops, warehouses and factories and a quantity and variety of material can be obtained in this way. Such things as cardboard, plastic and polystyrene containers are often readily supplied by general stores; waste metal turnings, stampings, filings and imperfect articles from factories; off-cuts of glass, plastics, wood, hardboard and broken tiles from builders' merchants, and large hoarding posters from poster service firms. Usually the parents represent a wide cross-section of the service and manufacturing industries, and having a vested interest in the education of their children they can be a most generous source of supply. Communication between the school and home is therefore essential. The children themselves are always only too ready to collect many of the found objects either in their own time or on organised searches. The availability of a pool of art materials is such a major factor in the development of so much creative work that it should be a matter of school concern and organisation, rather than an enterprise of individual teachers.

The problem of storage is often cited as the main objection to acquiring large stocks of materials. If the school buildings provide insufficient storage, use might be made of an idea adopted by a teacher who purchased a wooden garden shed, and sited it close to the school. The local education authority may be helpful here; approaches should be made through the appropriate adviser. Sometimes money can be provided out of the school fund, or an enterprising parent/teachers association may raise funds for such a project.

Supplementary equipment

The extra materials that the teacher provides will depend on the exact nature of the work, the collage materials used, and the scale of the work. If the assemblage is made up of papers or very thin card, then sugar paper or cardboard will be adequate for a base; *Polycell* or a wallpaper paste would be a strong enough adhesive. Lightweight materials in low relief such as seeds, shells, leaves, need to be arranged on a card or strawboard base. A glue such as *Gloy Multiglue* or *Marvin Medium* would be suitable. It is the heavier materials such as scrap metal, mechanical parts, plastics, glass and wood, that present more difficult problems, and therefore require more ingenuity and skill in fixing and joining. A firm, fairly rigid base such as hardboard, plywood, chipboard or thick fibreboard would be suitable. Strong adhesives are essential; *Multiglue* or *Marvin Medium* may be sufficient where good surface contact can be made, but heavy materials such as scrapyard junk in high relief may need a contact adhesive such as *Evostik* or *Bostik* or even an epoxy resin. Sometimes, because of the irregular shape or weight of an object, more elaborate methods of fixing may have to be employed, such as nailing, screwing or piercing the board and wiring the object to the surface. Some materials eg glass, plastics, stones, brick, coal, broken crockery or ceramic tiles may be satisfactory to use if they are set into a quick drying mastic or cement or *Polyfilla* base. As in junk modelling there are no set solutions, and success requires initiative and ingenuity.

Using the materials

The starting point for collage is often the materials which the child chooses because they inspire or interest him. Through trial and error he makes an arrangement which he finds satisfactory. Even this, the simplest approach to collage making, may be an absorbing learning situation. The arrangements and patterns that may be produced are infinite.

Often the materials present the child with ready-made images, for example a petal becomes a butterfly wing, shells or leaves a thorax and abdomen, berries become eyes, twigs become legs. The image-producing qualities of natural and some man-made junk give rise to all kinds of imaginative compositions. Some may be small and precious while others may occupy a much larger area. The approaches discussed so far arise from interactions between the child and the materials, and as learning processes take their place alongside other sensory exploratory experiences. However, it may be that children presented with mountains of junk, although fascinated by it, are also very confused by the wide choice offered. The teacher often needs to restrict the choice.

Ideas for designs may spring from many sources. First-hand visual experience of the local environment, or studies made in museums or the zoo provide excellent starting points. A close study of the arrangement, shape or pattern of objects will provide a ready made framework, or design, for the assemblage of collected objects and materials. Other areas of the curriculum may provide starting points, although in these instances children will be translating from pictorial reference material into collage.

Having arrived at a design it is necessary to transfer it to the card or board to be used as a base. The next stage is to work out which combination of materials is suitable for the sections of the design. This may be approached quite freely and intuitively. The child completes an area, and by trying other materials in surrounding areas decides on their suitability. Sometimes, however, more controlled methods are employed in which the units are carefully sorted and graded according to size, colour or tone. In this way subtle and elaborate pieces of work can be produced. The possible combinations of materials are endless and can involve children for long periods.

The value of collage

Collecting and handling the materials is in itself a worthwhile activity. It helps feed the child's natural curiosity about the world around him. If the teacher spends time in discussion about the location, distribution and manufacture of these items, this will lead to all kinds of discoveries about the nature and properties of substances from which interesting work in environmental studies, mathematics and science may result. Materials could be grouped together, mounted, labelled and displayed on the wall or discovery table.

The child, given the opportunity to select and handle unfamiliar materials, is being offered the chance to develop his awareness of tactile sensation and his sensitivity to shape, colour and texture.

The element of problem-solving is an important component of collage work even when approached at its simplest level. Some natural and man-made materials are so evocative that they present the child with ready made images; often when looking through a pile of junk the child will pick out certain pieces that strongly remind him of parts of animals, birds, insects, people, vehicles or buildings. This will be the beginning of a collage which can be developed or elaborated by the addition of other pieces. This gives heightened point to the subsequent search for additional units and makes the activities purposeful. In this way the child is using collage materials as an imaginative vehicle. The use of found objects or materials may be an approach to creative work which gives many children the confidence to go on to work with materials which demand more skill and inventiveness.

The older the child the more he is likely to require stimulation from the teacher. In this area, as in others, no teacher organising art work should operate without constant reference to first-hand visual experience. The patterns to be seen on natural and man-made things provide the framework for much exciting work in collage, and the search and setting down of visual ideas involves the development of recording skills, and the planning of work in stages. Elaborate assemblage will often involve a high degree of control. Pieces will have to be carefully sorted into containers and graded. Fixing units to a surface may require patience and control over a long period. Using hard or high relief materials may present difficult problems of fixing and joining two surfaces together, and their solutions may call for the development of new skills. Often fixing problems are so difficult that other children will have to assist. In fact one criterion for doing group work would be that the tool skills or handling problems are beyond the capabilities of the individual child and might be more successfully organised on a group basis. Collage, however, does allow for personal statements of a highly individual kind.

24 Collage by an eleven year old girl

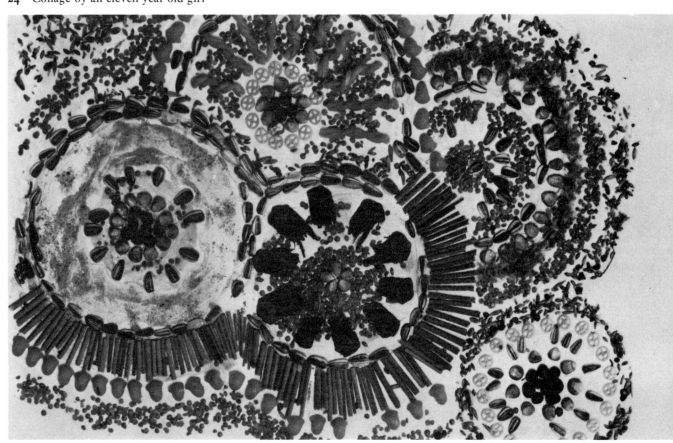

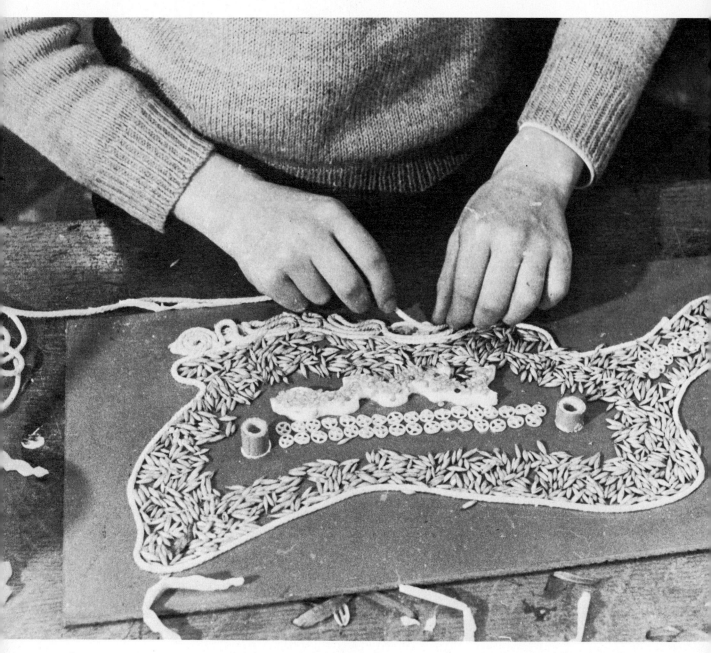

25 Even the simplest approaches
to collage present a child
with an absorbing learning situation

26 Butterfly collage
by a seven year old girl

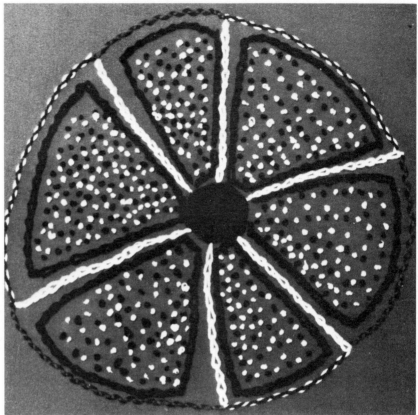

27 Collage by an eleven year old girl

28 String collage by a twelve year old girl

PRINTING AND ALLIED PROCESSES

Print-making is the transferring of a thin film of ink or pigment from one surface to another. Defining it in this way emphasises its essential feature as a discovery process concerning the character of surfaces – for above all, this is what is involved in making a print – whether it is made by an infant with a cut potato or a printer with an elaborate press.

Simple forms of printing

A simple form of printing consists of applying paint or ink to cut vegetables and various junk objects – blocks of wood, cardboard boxes, plastic containers, leaves, metal objects such as lids and wheels – and then pressing or stamping the inked object onto a surface. Infants are happy to pursue this activity and look eagerly for new objects to subject to this discovery process. It is not always possible to forecast the imprint that an object will give, and in taking a print or impression one gains a new awareness of its shape and surface quality. This is often surprising and for young children especially, a source of delight.

The application of ink or paint can be made in a number of ways. The easiest and most direct way is to apply paint such as powder colour with an ordinary hog-hair brush. For some purposes the viscosity of the pigment needs to be increased, and this is done by the addition of a water-based adhesive such as *Gloy* or any of the vinyl media such as *Multi-glue* or *Marvin Medium*. Cold-water *Polycell* is also suitable. This increased viscosity is particularly helpful if attempts are being made to print from metallic surfaces which have little affinity with water-based pigments.

For small objects the 'ink-pad' principle is worth following. Children can make ink-pads with a pad of felt, or plastic foam, or even folded sheeting or blotting paper in a tin or a saucer. Inks or dyes are poured on to this pad. Many prints can then be made easily and rapidly. Potatoes and other vegetables, wood and cork are particularly suitable for this method but it is less successful with hard, metallic objects which need a more tacky medium to adhere to their surface.

Decorators' foam rollers may also be used to 'ink-up' objects for printing and these have their value if the objects are fairly large – eg pieces of plank or plastic containers such as cress-boxes. The use of the ink-pad and the roller are fundamental techniques which can be developed later into more sophisticated techniques for fabric printing and graphic work.

Developments

The initial stages just described invariably focus on the individual print or impression. A child 'collects' such prints and after a session at this activity he finishes up with sheets of prints which are evidence of his concern to find and print as many objects as possible. There are two obvious developments from this stage, one into the building up of images through an accumulation of impressions, and the other into pattern making. An image may be suggested by the nature of the impressions being made – perhaps a print from a piece of wood suggests a dog's head, or a group of impressions from a cork suggest a texture of scales or feathers. Alternatively, given an idea, children could search for the appropriate objects to create the image they want. The second alternative, the development into pattern, is of considerable importance. The essential requirement is that children cease their search for new objects and select two or three from those they have already used, which they then use in combination. The emphasis goes from the individual imprint to the relationship between them and to what happens as they are repeated. However intuitively it may be, children are beginning to consider the spaces between imprints as well as the imprint itself and this is an important step forward. *Pattern depends on organisation*. This can be very simple – stripes for example – but children need to be given some 'rules of the game'. These may be derived from looking at objects in the environment. Stacks of bricks, pipes, tiles, pots, give a simple basis for pattern. Ploughed fields, corrugated iron, tigers, zebras, stacked wood, tracks in snow or sand, give ideas of stripes; seed heads, flower centres, wheels, photomicrographs, give ideas for patterns which grow concentrically around a centre. Children of all ages enjoy simple fundamental pattern and can become aware of it in their everyday environment.

In making pattern of this sort there is a tendency for units to be so widely spaced that they swim around on large areas of white. Two ideas are useful here; one is to suggest to children that prints should touch on at least one side and the second is to use a coloured paper which is more sympathetic to work on. It is not necessary to buy expensive papers for this purpose since they can easily be made by putting a simple wash of colour on newsprint, sugar or tempera paper. It is useful to have two 25 mm (1 in.) painting brushes for this sort of job, or decorator's rollers can be used. These methods produce individual coloured papers which are more subtle and more personal than bought ones. If they are printed on when they are still slightly damp they take a very sensitive image.

Printing of this sort is very sensitive to the nature of the surface *under* the printing paper. Often children attempt to print with their paper on a shiny *Formica* type table top. Vegetable blocks and junk objects very rarely have a completely flat surface and it is essential that some form of padding should be beneath the printing paper. The simplest and cheapest is an old magazine which has not been folded or crumpled. It is advisable to collect a pile of suitable magazines and to keep them for this purpose alone.

The greatest fault in simple printing arises from overloading the block. Children should be taught to avoid over inking and shown how to recognise when this is happening by the characteristic unevenness of the image with a dark, wet build-up along the edges. Blobby, uneven printing is just bad technique and it is not trespassing on a child's essential freedom to teach him to gain control over a medium, nor is he helped to develop by having poor quality

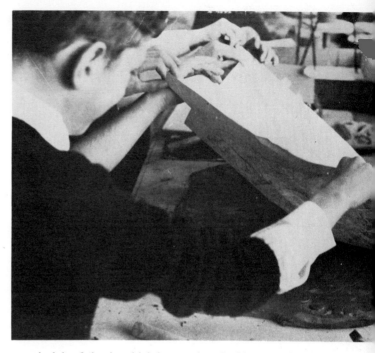

29 A slab of clay in which impressions had been made was used as a block for making prints

work accepted without a comment. The basis of good craftsmanship should be laid early, and too often one sees printing from upper juniors which shows little development from infant work.

An allied process is one in which impressions are made direct into slabs of clay instead of using paint on paper. This is discussed at the end of the chapter on three-dimensional work where the intention is to use the clay as the basis for a cast or to fire it – the link with this section is that such a slab of impressed clay can be used to print from. If a roller is used to ink-up the slab, a sheet of thin paper can then be laid over the clay and carefully burnished to produce a print. This is often worth doing even if the intention is to cast or fire the clay, for the residue of ink will either tint the cast or burn away in the kiln. See figure 29.

49

Other forms of printing

The first major technical step to print-making proper is the use of printing inks and special rollers with which to spread the ink, first on a tile and then on what from now on will be called the 'block' – although this term does not imply elaborate lino blocks and can still include the simplest found object. Printing ink differs from paint in being much more viscous. It is capable of being spread in a fine even film, able to resist drying out too quickly and is sticky enough to transfer itself under pressure from one surface to another. Generally speaking it is better to buy printing inks and not attempt to modify various paints to meet the needs. Water-based printing inks have obvious advantages over oil-based inks. Blocks and tools can be easily cleaned and the prints dry fairly quickly.

Printing rollers are usually of plastic or rubber; they vary in width from 65 mm to 180 mm or 230 mm ($2\frac{1}{2}$ in. to 7 or 9 in.) and in diameter from 25 mm to 75 mm (1 in. to 3 in.). Small rollers are of little use. It is best to buy the largest and the widest diameter rollers that can be afforded – 180 mm (7 in.), 38 mm ($1\frac{1}{2}$ in.) diameter are ideal general purpose rollers for the older juniors. For the younger children 100 mm (4 in.) rollers might be easier to use.

Mono printing

The simplest introduction to print-making with these materials is through the mono-print technique. A small quantity of printing ink is squeezed out onto a sheet of glass, a tile, a piece of hardboard, *Formica*, lino – anything in fact which has a flat, non-absorbent surface, although glass is probably the ideal material. The ink is spread with the roller to produce an even film of colour over the whole of the surface of the block. It is necessary to roll in a number of directions and helpful to let the roller lift off the block and spin at the end of a stroke in order to ensure an even coating.

If a sheet of paper is placed down on the block and carefully burnished it should peel off to reveal a simple area of colour. If, however, the ink is disturbed in any way by scratching, wiping, diluting with spots of water, or if pieces of paper are dropped onto it, then the printing area will show the results. Having done this process once, a second print can be taken from the same block, but because most of the ink has already been taken off by the first print, it will be paler. Other prints can be taken but they will be progressively paler. Because it is impossible to take two identical prints from the block this process is termed 'mono-printing'. This offers many opportunities for inventiveness and exploration. For instance having taken two prints, the block can then be cleaned up and inked with a different colour. It is then taken up carefully, turned over and put down on top of the first print. To carry out the burnishing process the block and paper should be carefully drawn to the edge of the table where it can be turned over again and the paper burnished. When the paper is peeled off, areas which were masked off reveal the first colour, on areas left white from the first printing the second colour is pure, the remaining areas show the second colour printed on top of the first. Thus from two printings three colours result. The process can be repeated as many times as patience and interest permit. It will often be found, however, that after three printings, unless the print is allowed to dry, ink is leaving the paper and transferring to the block. This reversing of the process suggests another possibility and one could take such a wet print and by pressing down on it with junk objects or wood blocks deliberately remove the top layer(s) of ink to reveal the under colours.

Successive prints need not be placed accurately one on top of another. Different shapes and forms can be printed together – either alongside each other, or on top of each other, or in any combination of these. There is no process in the whole range of visual arts activities which offers so wide a scope for invention with such simple techniques. Once the principle is grasped, children are able to invent their own methods. The important thing is to get them to move into the second stage of over-printing where the really exciting things begin to happen and in which they get an experience of colour which cannot be obtained through any other process.

Printing from blocks

Mono-printing leads on to further developments. Blocking out areas by inserting paper masking, thus leaving white spaces in the print, is clearly a lead into lino cutting, in which removing the surface of the block is the equivalent process. It might be worth while using a piece of lino for mono-printing before going on to use the same piece to make a cut block – and no reason why, having begun to cut the block, all the mono-print techniques of scraping and masking should not continue to be used.

An alternative development is to take, for instance, hardboard as the basis for a block and stick things on – cardboard, string, foil, cloth, anything which is not too different in height from the other materials used. These collage blocks offer further opportunity for discovery and invention. If material as thin as card is stuck down on the block, the background as well as the card will pick up the ink and the printed effect will be that of a white 'halo' around the card motifs. Unless the materials stuck down are sufficiently high for the roller to bridge the gap between various parts of the block, the background will always pick up some ink and similarly the paper will sink between the raised parts and pick up this same background ink. This is not a fault but a characteristic of this particular approach and is an effect to be exploited.

Printing from lino blocks is well known, but the particular techniques are often taught in isolation and much of the real excitement of print-making is lost. Basically there are two approaches to using lino – a linear/texture approach and an area approach. If lino is used, after exploration of the sort that has been under discussion it is likely that the area approach will be followed. That is to say, the pupil will be concerned with areas of colour and their relationship to each other and with the effects of over-printing. If, however, children are given lino and cutting tools early on in their experience of print-making, their first impulse is to cut in line; in effect, to incise a line drawing. This is not wrong but a natural stage in their progress and is often true of the first attempts of adults without previous experience. Linear concepts appear to be more fundamental than colour/area concepts and so, without previous experience directed towards an area approach, it is to be expected that line drawing will occur. The development of this work is by enrichment of the linear cutting through the exploration of textural effects. Drawings with a strong textural content, eg drawings of buildings with roofs, textured walls, cobbled streets, bushes and trees, can be translated into textures made by the tools and so enrich the overall effect of the block. Such prints are best printed in black on white paper or alternatively in white on black paper. An interesting technique pioneered by Edward Bawden is to take a number of prints from the same block in different coloured inks on a variety of coloured papers. Then, taking one print as the master-print, cut up the others and paste parts down on the master. This collage approach can produce a rich colour effect from very limited means, and of course, since everything has come from the one block, every part will fit.

A group of young secondary school boys were taken to a science museum in which there was a fine collection of vintage and veteran cars, which the boys drew in pencil or ink. On returning to school each boy made a direct translation of his drawing on to a lino cut and it was suggested that all the background lino be cut away, leaving the car as an isolated motif. These were then used in two ways:

1 They were printed on paper to make Christmas cards
2 The blocks were printed on fabric in horizontal stripes to create a group fabric

The cuts varied in size, in textural qualities, in the viewpoint taken of the car, and in the colour chosen to print, and the total effect was very satisfying as a fabric and provided the group with a considerable sense of achievement. Similar work has also been done with nine to ten year olds taking buildings in a nearby street as the starting point and translating drawings directly into linear lino-cuts with some textural developments. Any form of cut block is likely to be richer and more successful if it begins from some study or strong visual experience, for the attempt to translate the experience into the new and difficult medium is the spur to technical exploration, and offers a continuous process of decision-making at an intuitive level, if not at a higher level of consciousness.

There are many books on print-making and this is not the place for a technical exposition – indeed the essence of what has been said is that there are very few technicalities involved in printing and that technique should be invented and personal.

The value of printing

Relief printing is a simple technical process which offers a rich and satisfying experience through which a child can develop his personal imagery or work abstractly without being self-conscious. The child is free to invent his own techniques and to make decisions about the way work will develop without reference to a set procedure. Although it can be started at a very simple level, printing can be elaborated and developed to a high technical standard. In this way it lays the foundation for the development of craftsmanship which is based on understanding of materials and tools and a sympathetic response to them. Finally it offers an experience of colour which is unobtainable through any other process, for the effects produced by over-printing and various textural qualities are unique to printing.

Allied developments

Although different in principle, *screen printing* ought perhaps to be considered in conjunction with relief printing since it can be combined with it if desired. Screen printing is a form of stencilling in which the parts of the stencil are stuck to a fine mesh of cotton organdie, silk, or nylon, stretched over a frame. Children can start by using simple stencilling methods. As with junk printing, this can begin by using found objects with holes in them or with interesting edges which can be stencilled around. Once again the child is involved in discovering. The teacher may have to provide some of the initial stimuli but once children have become interested they will themselves take up the search for unusual objects. Cartons are useful starting points. Of particular value are the ingenious packages used for Easter eggs, which, when opened out flat are astonishingly complicated and can provide the most intriguing patterns if stencilled in stripes. Other sources are gaskets from engines of cars, various small metal parts such as parts of a lock, keys, industrial waste such as metal stampings or leather scrap from shoe factories. Sometimes the objects collected will not of themselves be useable as stencils but by placing them on stiff paper, tracing round the shape and then cutting it out, a simple stencil can be produced which will stand up to a considerable amount of printing.

Stencilling can be done with paint brushes, special stencil brushes, rag dipped in paint, sponges, paint rollers, pastels or crayons, sprayers – anything in fact which transfers pigment to a surface.

It is an easy step from this to using a screen. For most children in the age range under consideration it is probably best to have prepared screens with a standard opening of say 30 cm (12 in.) by 38 cm (15 in.). The reserved area of the screen is best varnished so that it is waterproofed and capable of standing up to wear and tear. Pupils can then cut paper masks to use under such screens. If the mask is put down on the printing paper, the screen placed in position and the first pull taken, the ink itself will cause the mask to adhere to the screen when it is lifted, so that the process can be repeated as often as desired. The usual method of making a screen print is to use a squeegee, but decorator's rollers are easier to use for young children and give reasonable results. See figure 34. It also means that one need not use special screen inks but fabric dyestuffs or *Polycell* and paint.

In developing motifs for screen printing all that has been said about ideas for simple stencilling is still applicable. A further possibility is to use shadows as the basis for a paper stencil. For this a good strong light source is required which will throw sharply defined shadows on a convenient surface upon which one can pin the paper that is being used for making the masks. Pupils can examine the shapes of a number of objects – natural forms such as bracken, thistles, sprays of leaves, feathers; man-made forms such as mincers, presses, lamps; models such as *Meccano* or *Dinky* toys; staplers – the list is endless and, as with printing from objects, to study shadows is to discover new qualities of shape and form in the objects studied. If the projected shadow is of a suitable size, a pupil can draw or paint the actual shadow on the paper and use this directly to make the stencil by cutting out the appropriate parts. Alternatively the pupil can make a drawing in which the shadow is increased or reduced in scale.

A similar approach would be to use slides projected directly onto the masking paper. These slides can be made by sandwiching thin material between the glass of slide holders such as one can obtain from photographic shops. Feathers, small seeds, leaves, flower petals, grasses, ink, paint, oil and ink, paper, can be experimented with to produce surprising images. An overhead projector might be used in a similar way to produce experimental images which could be developed as simple screen prints. For older children, who may be less confident about their drawing, this type of approach involves them in image construction in a novel way which enlists their interest without raising the inhibitions which are associated with more traditional drawing and painting.

30 Print patterns made with an ice-cream stick

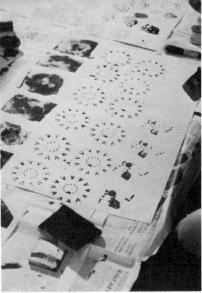

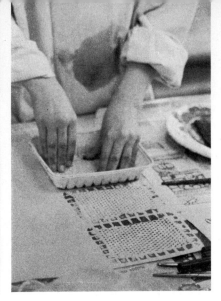

31 Printing from a found object

32 A sheet of impressions

33 Printing from a plastic container

34 Screen printing with a decorator's roller

35 Printing from a cress box

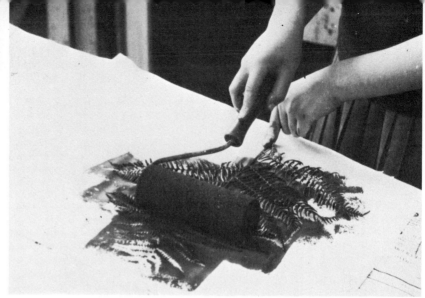

36 Rolling ink over a fern with a decorator's roller

37 A lino print

WORK WITH THREE-DIMENSIONAL MATERIALS

Traditionally children's work in the visual arts has been largely confined to two-dimensional materials such as paints and crayons. Although now a certain amount is being done with clay, and junk materials are being used for constructions, three-dimensional activities are often little understood and therefore limited in their objectives. They are frequently regarded as model-making linked to project work, or unstructured 'free expression' activities. Neither of these are without value, but a real understanding of what three-dimensional materials can offer to the development of a child could lead to better use being made of the opportunities for original work involving not only spontaneous expression but also a good deal of thought.

Different ranges of material offer clearly distinguishable types of experience. Basically material is either used in a constructional way or its shape is changed by carving, if it is hard, or by modelling if it is of a soft malleable nature. Three-dimensional work is discussed here under these three basic headings: constructing, carving and modelling.

CONSTRUCTION

This section is divided into two parts: one on constructions made from materials that stimulate the imagination, and the second on constructions made from formal materials.

1 Materials which stimulate the imagination

Children have a natural desire to collect objects and fragments which have excited their interest or held some significance for them. This interest in found objects is the basis for three-dimensional work of an imaginative kind, for children easily invest objects with significance and incorporate them into imaginative play. For this to happen an object must suggest some outstanding characteristic of the thing imagined, or be sufficiently ambiguous in form to allow images to be projected onto it. This apparently innate tendency to invest ambiguous forms with meaning – to see them for what they are *not* – is not confined to childhood. It is a basic attribute of our perceptive mechanism which strives to organise our sensations into orderly patterns which we can understand. It is, however, a human attribute of which we make too little use in art education.

Sources

Most environments are rich sources of materials which provide a variety of texture, colour, shape, scale and those properties which are fundamental to particular materials – eg tensile strength, warmth or coldness to touch, soft/hard variations. As well as this, the action of weathering and other natural forces can give found objects strange and exciting qualities which have a romantic appeal to children. Obvious places to collect such materials are the beach and the river-bed. Schools in industrial areas have their own possibilities: waste or scrap yards, or even the local rubbish tip, can provide strange and exciting finds. Factories supply many different scrap materials. What is required is an imaginative attitude on the part of the teacher which will fire the children to collect from all sorts of sources objects and materials of strange and unexpected character.

Use of the materials

If the materials offer a wide range of ambiguous forms and have interesting textures and colours, they will provide strong stimuli to the child. The role of the teacher here is to discuss what images the materials suggest. Once the child has invested a shape with the characteristics of a particular image, he will then search for other pieces to enable him to elaborate his idea. In this way materials take on a dual role; they exist as pieces of drift wood or containers with their own special identity of shape and colour, but when joined together with other pieces they are transformed into a new image.

Sometimes the teacher may provide a theme which will direct the child to search for materials which fit the particular idea. Once the child has started a model, the teacher will discuss how the work can be developed. Creativity is more than just producing new ideas. The ability to develop and elaborate is an important aspect of creative work.

It is important for the teacher to be aware of what the materials can offer and to structure the children's activities to give them what they need in the way of formative experience. For example, *where* the work takes place will largely determine the scale of what is made, irrespective of what the materials available might offer in the way of possibilities. There can be an advantage in working outside or even at the location on which materials are to be found, for instance the beach, where the scale of work can be very large. Working inside tends to mean the work will be small in scale, but this is not necessarily a bad thing. Small scale work, especially if it is individual work, is often extremely sensitive and delicate. Alternatively large scale work offers scope for group co-operation and provides a sense of achievement which cannot easily be obtained in other ways.

Supplementary materials

However many different materials an environment offers it is likely that the teacher will need to provide supplementary materials. For example, strings and wires of various gauges, perhaps plywood and offcuts of timber, chicken wire, metal foils, various sorts of cloth, leather scraps, beads and buttons are among things which might be built up as permanent resources. The teacher has also to be imaginative in the range of tools and adhesives provided. Problems arise mostly from the need to join one material to another rather than cutting or shaping, and these problems are usually without traditional ready-made solutions. This is an important aspect of the work and one which develops in children the capacity to improvise and to develop their own techniques rather than to rely on adult know-how. Adhesives need to be good multi-purpose glues of the contact type, capable of holding many types of materials together, with perhaps an adhesive suitable for paper, card and fabric which need not be quite so powerful. Nails, screws, pins, staples, needles and thread and thin wire, together with the appropriate tools, are required to enable children to tackle most of the problems of joining.

The value of imaginative materials

Work with these materials is not only creative in the sense that children are developing unique images which arise out of their personal response to materials, but also productive of many problems for which there are no set solutions. The solving of these is an important creative activity, but it can also involve children in valuable social situations in that the discussion of a problem with the teacher or other pupils is a contact which might not otherwise have arisen. It brings the teacher in as someone with experience to tap rather than the authority who gives the correct solution. The changed role of the teacher in such situations enables the child to assume responsibility for his own work and to grow in self confidence. The sense of achievement which arises from creating something new and imaginative is a most rewarding experience.

Constructing with three-dimensional materials of what may be called the evocative or latent image type offers children a wide range of tactile and kinaesthetic experience, which is the basis for that knowledge of materials essential for the development of craftsmanship later on. It provides opportunities for the development of ingenuity and skill in the solving of unorthodox problems of joining things together. It offers a 'working situation' contact between teacher and pupil and helps to establish a different kind of relationship than that which is inherent in a formal teaching situation.

Children working in this way are capable of longer spans of attention than is normal and can be involved in pieces of work for a considerable length of time.

2 Formal materials

The distinction between image-producing materials and formal materials is a somewhat arbitrary one and in practice both types are likely to be available and used freely by children. It is clear, however, that there is a big difference in the responses called forth by say, a piece of drift wood and lengths of cut and planed timber, or between rusty metal tins gathered from the beach and a construction kit such as *Meccano*. Materials which consist of fairly standard, squared-up units invite close-fitting right-angle joints, and so lend themselves to the construction of what might be termed mechanical or architectural forms.

Much contemporary sculpture consists of constructions which use such formal material, and the objects produced are of a mechanical or architectural character; it is questionable, however, if such an approach is appropriate for children in the age range under consideration. Pupils taken to exhibitions will sometimes return to school and, as they say, 'do some modern art'; they are often merely aping the appearance of the work they have seen without any real understanding of what the artist has been trying to do. It is better for children to use such formal materials for constructions which have a clear functional purpose, for example an animal house or a play den, or a construction for play purposes such as a fort or a cockpit in an aeroplane. The imaginative use of large wooden building blocks for play constructions is a typical activity of the nursery and infant class and is too little developed in the junior school. In figure 47 a boy is constructing a fort which he wants to inhabit and shoot from. A similar approach is seen in drama work in which large rostra and other props are used as adjuncts to imaginative work.

The value of formal materials

Formal materials, unlike the evocative materials, do not readily awaken images – the image has, as it were, to be brought to the material. It is true, of course, that children will incorporate such formal materials, for example blocks of wood, into images that they are constructing, but the materials themselves have not given rise to the idea. The nature of formal materials – the fact that they are normally squared-up as blocks or planks or strips of metal – offers opportunities to children to explore *functional* rather than image-making problems. This is an important point for as soon as a child tackles a functional problem he has to accept criteria which are external to himself. In other words, the job has to work. This may be a very crude 'working' but it either fulfills certain requirements or it does not, and if it does not then imagination cannot fill the gap. A kite must fly, a *Meccano* model must lift or run on wheels, an animal cage must keep the animal secure. As well as this, the child has defined his objective before starting. In building an image the final result is not often defined and is subject to constant change; in setting out to build, say, a nesting box for a guinea pig, the problem has been defined, certain criteria have to be met and the child has thought about the job before he begins to think about materials.

Having set himself a problem, the child then begins to consider appropriate materials with which to solve it. Successful problem solving, however simple and crude, requires some knowledge of the nature of materials. Although children will not consciously reject say, metal in favour of wood, it is, in fact, their experience of these two materials and their ability to work them upon which their choices are made. And within the chosen material, there then arises a further range of decisions concerning size and strength.

Tackling functional problems gives rise to further need for discrimination and the development of skills; the joints in a functional job have to stand stress and strain, perhaps even to move or slide. Workmanship becomes a critical factor and the child, in order to achieve what he has set out to do, is led into acquiring new knowledge and skill with tools. He needs to be able to cut squarely, to drill holes accurately, to sew, to use glue of the right sort – indeed there are many skills of a fundamental nature which children can be led to acquire in this way. Craftsmanship may seem too grand a term to apply to the work of children but the basis for its later development is laid in the careful nurturing of sensitivity to materials and concern for their effective use through skill with tools and processes. The teacher's role is to provide the child with the encouragement and the opportunity to tackle 'real' functional jobs appropriate to his age and skills, and to provide the instruction in skills and processes as they become relevant. As children approach the top of the junior school or move upwards through a middle school, it may need more than one teacher to meet the demands of intelligent, active children who have been encouraged to work in this way. This is the case for specialist knowledge to be available in specific areas, such as art, needlecraft, domestic science, woodwork and metal work, but it is not a plea for specialist teaching of an old fashioned type, in which children were taught separate skills in a formal and often meaningless context. Children are anxious to acquire skills and respect skill when they meet it, but it is essential that they shall acquire them as and when they are relevant to their needs.

It can be a mistake to consider 'art' in too narrow a way. Teachers should aim to develop in children a sense of design and a capacity for aesthetic enjoyment arising from the use and contemplation of functional objects, just as much as they try to develop their visual awareness in other areas. The children's own involvement in the making is the foundation for this development of a design sense.

38   Children have a natural desire to collect objects which in some way arouse their interest

39   The child communicates her enthusiasm to an adult, who in turn enriches the child's knowledge

40 and **41**   Junk material

42 Rough materials can be used with delicacy and concern for accurate placing

43 This kind of work demands considered decisions

44 Working outside minimizes problems of noise and space

45 A variety of techniques can be employed to finish off a model. Here off-cuts of wood and paint are used

46 When children work in groups or pairs the opportunities for discussion are a valuable part of the process. Group work generally means larger scale work

47 A fort constructed with formal materials

CARVING

Carving presents children with a totally different experience from any other kind of three-dimensional work. In contemporary sculpture sophisticated tools and processes are used to produce images which are appropriate to our age, but traditionally, and certainly with pre-adolescent children, carving is carried out with hand tools to make an image which gradually develops as the work progresses.

Materials

Children require carving materials which are fairly soft and allow them to work without excessive effort or risk. For young children soap, salt, green-clay (unfired clay, eg unfired bricks from the local brick works), insulation blocks of various types, are materials which can be worked reasonably quickly and easily. Older children could use wood or stone, which offer opportunities for more precise work and a good finish to the surface. This latter point is of particular importance for young teenagers who are often prepared to devote considerable time and effort to the perfection of a beautiful surface. Alabaster, which can sometimes be obtained locally, is particularly rewarding in this respect.

The carved image

Much of the material available for carving comes in the form of rectangular blocks and this presents certain problems to the inexperienced carver. Faced with such material the typical response is to project a *two-dimensional* image on to one of the surfaces and then cut backwards into the block. In some cases children will work backwards from all four faces of a block so that four images are produced – each unrelated to the others and presenting peculiar problems as they approach each other towards the centre of the block. Older children manage to move more easily from this starting point to a full three-dimensionality, but even so

such carving tends to be very stiff and has something of the quality of a 'thick silhouette'.

One way to solve this problem is to offer children material which is *not* in rectangular blocks. Faced with an irregular lump of material it is much easier to 'see' an image in the form already there than it is to see an image imprisoned in a rectangular prism. The carving then becomes the development of what is seen to be in existence already, and it can develop with a sensitivity to the qualities of the material and its projections and hollows, which is very different from working into a brick-like shape. Because there is a free development from the configurations already existing, an element of distortion can enter, which is both acceptable to the carver and personal in that it is his or her response to a particular set of possibilities.

Once a carving is past the initial flat stage and a child is beginning to contend with the problems of creating a three-dimensional image experience from non-visual sources may be used. Our knowledge of, for example, our own heads is derived from the sight of others, from our own reflection, from our body sensations and movements, and above all from our own handling of our heads when we eat, brush our teeth, comb our hair, hold our head in our hands. The relationships known to us through this sort of experience are different from those derived from sight. For example, we are far more aware of our faces from our eyes downwards than we are of our heads above our eyes. The common image for a face which sets the eyes far too high may arise from this sense of proportion which is not based on vision. Similarly, the characteristic indentations which often stand for eyes in primitive carving, whether made by children or from primitive cultures, are true to our sensation of eyes as holes through which we look out to the world – or into other people. Carving, and modelling too (see page 70), reflect fundamental experience of form in a way which is not always found in two-dimensional work.

The value of carving

The essential quality of carving is its decisiveness; unlike clay work, what is removed is irreplaceable. In carving therefore one has to commit oneself to a definite action. This presents problems for the inexperienced carver of any age where three-dimensional schemata are undeveloped and he is unable to visualise the results of his action. First carvings are often tentative and evolve from two-dimensional images projected onto, and cut into, flat surfaces. Carving like all three-dimensional work, develops an understanding of three-dimensional form, but because of the intractable nature of the materials used and the slow process involved, the child has to respect the inherent qualities of the material and their effect upon his image. The difficulties of this process can provide the child with a challenge and a sense of adventure and achievement which is unsurpassed in any other area of work. Whilst carving is an activity which can be done by pupils of any age it should be obvious that younger children are more likely to achieve satisfaction with easily worked materials, whilst the young adolescent may respond to the challenge of alabaster or oak with the greater skill and strength required to work them. These more permanent materials allow children to bring the surface to a high degree of finish, and they can derive great satisfaction from burnishing and refining the forms they have carved. This sensitivity to surface quality is an important aspect of carving.

48 Carving presents children with a totally different kind of experience from any other three-dimensional work

49–56 The different stages in carving a man out of an unfired brick by a six year old boy

57 A soft material such as soap provides a good introduction to carving for the young child

58 Another soft material that allows children to work without undue effort or risk can be found in thermal insulation blocks

59 Children develop skill and sensitivity without the need for sophisticated tools

60 Plaster, cast into irregular shapes by pouring the wet mixture into polythene bags, offers children a suitable carving material

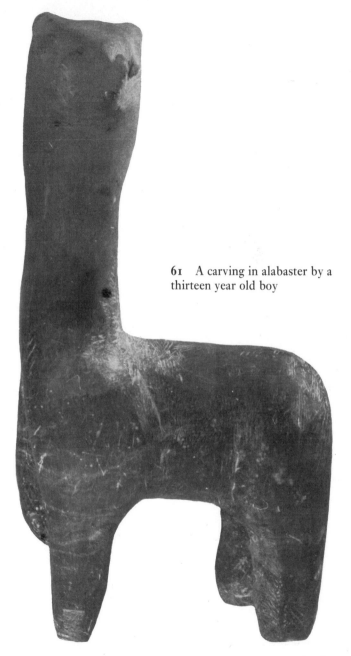

61 A carving in alabaster by a thirteen year old boy

MODELLING

Plastic materials, especially clay, are unique in their capacity to respond to every nuance of physical contact; they can record the most delicate approach to the surface on which finger tips leave a subtle patina of impressions, or they can give evidence of the most violent attack, in which the material has been gripped and squeezed to produce tortured forms which are expressive of the movements which created them. As in drawing and painting, these materials offer an immediate record of action, of our physical contact with the medium. This immediacy is a source of satisfaction and the reason for involvement with them which is more than simply the involvement of making images.

Early experiences with plastic materials
The child's first experiences of plastic materials occur when he experiments with the semi-solid foods presented to him. Bread, sponge cake, pudding and many other foods are squashed and squeezed with both interest and satisfaction. Some children continue this sort of experience with mud and earth and sand as they become old enough to move around and entertain themselves with the materials of the garden or yard. Many children however, are deprived of such fundamental sensory experience. They are confined to high flats or town houses where opportunities do not exist, or they are prevented by parental attitudes from indulging in these activities. For such children it is especially important that provision be made for them to use clay and *Plasticine* or similar products. These materials provide children with rich experiences which can be gained from no other source.

For many children plastic materials provide unique opportunities to explore and make sense of their ever expanding world. Often their models will be of people or

62   *The boat race* by a six year old boy

animals caught up in a particular situation where they exhibit the qualities of good or evil, strength or weakness, passiveness or aggression. For instance, one child made a model consisting of some forty figures who formed two tug-of-war teams. String was used for the rope. The poses of the figures and the accompanying commentary left no doubt that the child was undergoing a deeply satisfying experience. After seeing the Boat Race on television, a six year old produced the model illustrated in figure 62. In the *Plasticine* models of soldiers in battle in figure 63, ingenious use is made of 'odds and ends' – hair grips, safety pins, nails. Another child was observed forming figures around a large round stone. The stone had assumed gigantic proportions in the child's mind, and the people were trying to

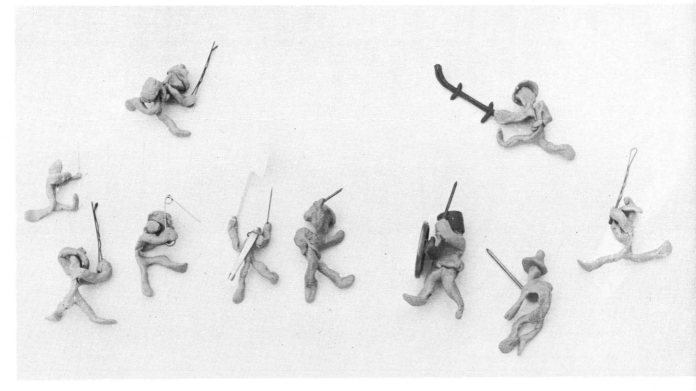

63 *Soldiers in battle* by a six year old boy

push it along. Yet another had made a human chain suspended from a table edge to the floor. The table became a mountain and the people had formed themselves into a ladder to escape from a bog.

Young children are less concerned with the visual appearance of the objects they have created than with their play potential. Children given opportunities for work with plastic materials gradually develop an interest in the more formal elements of three-dimensional models.

Non-visual experience
Three-dimensional plastic materials allow the creation of images which are equivalents for non-visual experience.

Our knowledge of three-dimensional form, and especially our knowledge of our own bodies, is based to a large extent on tactile and kinaesthetic experience which is fragmentary, distorted and subjective, in comparison with visual experience. Our culture, however, exerts strong pressures to encourage the production of images which are objective – that is to say, images which are consistent with photographic images. There is, however, considerable evidence to suggest that not all people can or do see in this way, and that many people, if not pressurised to conform to the photographic norm, would create images which drew on this non-visual reservoir of experience and were, as a result, personal and subjective.

To create such apparently distorted images in two-dimensional work becomes difficult if a pupil makes comparisons between his or her work and that of adults who conform to the general 'realistic' norm. When working in three-dimensional materials, however, this predisposition towards non-visual experience is less easily suppressed and the subsequent distortion is more easily accepted.

Three-dimensional schemata

Most children evolve two-dimensional schemata for the representation of people, houses, animals, etc, and also for the relationship between them, as for instance, the baseline schema for the representation of space. Few people ever evolve three-dimensional schemata which attain the sophistication or consistency of their two-dimensional ones.

Conceiving in three dimensions is more than adding together 'x' number of two-dimensional images, and requires considerable experience of working in the round. Early work in clay, whatever the age of the worker, may have all the disjointed qualities that children's early two-dimensional work displays, in which they present information, but are unable to relate, for example, eyes to hair to head.

This can be seen clearly in an experiment carried out with college students. Half were asked to model their own heads, working blindfold, and the other half worked from sight. There were certain obvious and superficial differences: details such as eyelashes and wrinkles were missing from the 'blind' models; but what was striking was the basic similarity in the three-dimensional schema for the head. The proportions of the head – the exaggeration of the face at the expence of the rest of the head, the inability to place the ear correctly in relation to the face, the general lack of depth from face to ear, all showed a knowledge of the head's form based on touch and self-experience. This is clear evidence that when sighted persons are working in plastic materials the resultant forms are influenced by non-visual experience, and controlled by touch rather than sight.

The value of modelling

Children need constant opportunity to use *Plasticine* or clay as one important basis for play activity, both at home and in nursery and infant schools. During this period it may be found that *Plasticine* (in large packets) is a more satisfactory material than clay because it remains in a more or less plastic state, and unlike clay will not dry out when subjected to heat. It has been found, too, that after children have finished a particular activity they are usually quite happy to break up their models and start afresh next time, although the teacher should not insist that the children do so until they are ready.

The value of this medium is that through it the child can examine and begin to make sense of his everyday life. By using a plastic medium as part of his play activity, he can act out his fantasies and aggressions in a way which is meaningful.

These activities are of value to all children but particularly to those who have difficulty in adjusting their behaviour and emotional expression to social requirements. C. R. Rogers puts complete freedom of *symbolic* expression as an essential requirement for the development of creativity.

'To express in behaviour all feelings, impulses and formings may not in all instances be freeing. Behaviour may in some instances be limited by society, and this is as it should be. But symbolic expression need not be limited. Thus, to destroy a hated object . . . by destroying a symbol of it, is freeing. To attack it in reality may create guilt and narrow the psychological freedom which is experienced.'

Plastic materials offer children uniquely sensitive media which allow the most subtle and personal approaches and provide opportunities to develop three-dimensional schemata which represent a wide variety of experience.

It should be stressed that no one type of image is better than another. It is probable however, that the more three-dimensional work is visually controlled, the less likely it is to convey those qualities of personal vision which education in art seeks to develop. It is because work in all three-dimensional materials, not just the plastic ones, allows these more subjective qualities to be expressed that three-dimensional work has such a great deal to offer.

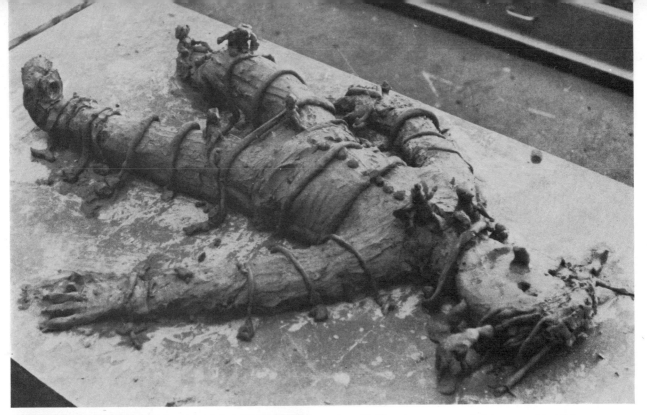

64 *Gulliver* by a group of eight year old children

65 *The old woman who lived in a shoe*
by two six year old girls

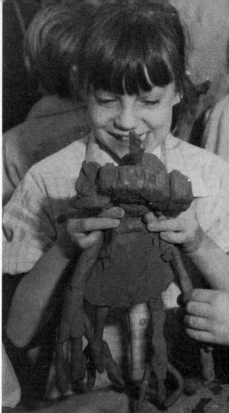

66 Clay used as a part of children's play activity allows them to act out their fantasies

67 Clay model by an eight year old girl

68 Clay offers an immediate record of the child's physical contact with the medium

RELATED APPROACHES

Clay as a relief medium

There is another way of using clay which has something in common with the making of mosaics and constructions, or printing using junk material – that is the using of a slab of clay to record the imprint of tools, fingers and objects. A clay slab provides an inviting surface upon which to make marks. The simplest of tools – pencils, pieces of wood of varying sizes, nails and screws, and found objects of every description, leave imprints of unexpected vitality and variety and the act of taking say, a bolt with a nut on and pressing it into the clay along its length is an act of discovery which never fails to intrigue children and adults. Simpler tools which leave circular or triangular indentations, etc can be made to assume exciting qualities when they are repeated in close succession, and it is easy to make rich surface textures in this way. As with using junk to make constructions, these impressions can easily be built up into images. For those children who find difficulty in drawing because they have lost confidence or have, as a result of poor teaching, assumed that they cannot draw, this approach with its often humorous 'unreal' quality gives them a new freedom and impetus to explore a different form of image making.

From making impressions in clay it is an easy step to adding clay shapes – pellets of clay pressed on in free manner, or the addition of carefully cut slab shapes. The illustrations show such an approach taken with a group of junior children who used pastry cutters among other tools to create this extraordinary rich pattern. This work was done in about an hour and a half and is testimony to the high degree of involvement that the activity generated. See figures 69–73.

Mosaic

A further area of creative work that can be explored, using mainly found materials, is the mosaic. Traditionally this refers to cut glass, ceramic or minerals set in slow drying mastic, but if this is extended to include a range of natural and man-made objects, a wide range of creative possibilities is opened up. Materials that could be used include shells, stones, glass, brick, coal, broken crockery, buttons, beads, plastics, bottle or jar tops, bark, driftwood, nutshells, cones, wood off-cuts, machine parts and metal scrap.

The traditional approach to mosaic making is often referred to as the indirect or reverse method. In using this approach the tesserae (the glass, ceramics, etc) are arranged, and paper glued on to the surface. When dry the mosaic is lifted and the back of the tesserae pressed into wet plastic or cement. Once the pieces are set, the paper is wetted and peeled off, leaving the even surface of the mosaic exposed.

This method has been used successfully with children of secondary school age, but with younger children a more direct method should be employed. The easiest way is to press mosaic pieces directly into wet cement. This method is so simple that with organisation and a few safeguards even children of lower junior age can do this work successfully. A strong base is essential. Chipboard or plywood are excellent materials. Ideally this should be about 9 mm ($\frac{3}{8}$ in.) thick for panels up to $1\frac{1}{4}$ m (4 ft) square and 15 mm ($\frac{5}{8}$ in.) for larger scale works. Hardboard, too, is suitable if the panel is given rigidity by the addition of a simple batten frame, glued or nailed to the edge of the panel. Later it can be painted to provide an attractive frame, bordering the finished work. Once the design has been drawn on the panel, work on the mosaic can begin.

One of the problems to be overcome is how to secure the mosaic firmly to the base. Bayonet tacks driven into the surface provide a 'key' for the mixture to grip. 12 mm ($\frac{1}{2}$ in.) tacks should be left projecting for about half their length. Another method is to use a staple gun. Again the staples should be left projecting from the surface. Those with long shanks are therefore better for this purpose.

If children are working in groups some of them could be involved in sorting and grading the mosaic pieces. The pieces can be selected according to their colour, size or shape, and put into jars or yoghurt containers. When the children have decided that a particular material is suitable for part of their design, then the cement can be mixed. Ordinary grey cement and builders' sand are suitable. These should be mixed in small quantities in a proportion of about 2 parts cement to 1 part sand. It is best to mix and spread only as much as can be covered with the mosaic pieces before it begins to dry out. The pieces should be pressed firmly into the cement so that only the surface is showing. A slower drying mixture can be made by incorporating hydrated lime (5 parts cement, 5 parts sand and 1 part hydrated lime). The resultant mixture is of a buttery texture and is therefore extremely easy to spread. The proportion of 10% lime, should, however, not be exceeded or the mixture remains dry and crumbly and will never set hard.

If coloured glass is used, the translucent quality of the material is seen to advantage if it is set into a white base material. White cement suitable for this purpose can be obtained from large builders' merchants. *Polyfilla* makes an excellent base material but may be too expensive for anything other than small areas. Plaster of paris is too soft to hold shiny pieces firmly. To contrast the jewel-like qualities of glass or crockery and patterned areas of stones, shells or buttons, a simple alternative approach can be used. This involves mixing together damp sawdust, glue (*Gloy* multiglue or heavy duty *Polycell*) and liquid or powder colour. These are mixed thoroughly until a wet crumbly substance is obtained and then spread evenly onto the base board. The mixture sets rock hard and large areas can be covered very quickly. If it is used to surround areas of mosaic made from found objects, the detailed areas stand out well against the simple background.

For mosaic a few basic tools only are required: kitchen knives or a small plasterer's trowel, a hammer, pliers, a tenon saw, jugs and a mixing bowl. This basic working approach to mosaic making has been used successfully with children of seven and eight years of age. Older children, having gained basic skills, will wish to experiment, and perhaps attempt to produce mosaics *in situ* on walls, floors

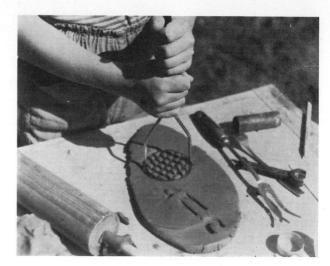

69–73 Exploring clay

or courtyards. Some of these however will require more sophisticated techniques and reference should be made to specialist books on the subject.

Mosaic is not a fluid medium, and does not allow the spontaneous expression of an idea like a brush loaded with pigment. But as a slow constructional process it is an activity which allows scope for group or individual work, using a simple craft-based approach which depends on a number of planned stages.

74 Materials are sorted according to their size, colour, shape or texture

75 Mosaic by a group of eight year old girls

76 Setting the mosaic pieces in a cement base

THE BACKWARD CHILD

Backward children are very often as backward in art as they are in every other aspect of the school curriculum. They lack the initiative, the confidence, the ability to concentrate, muscular control, and the intelligent understanding of processes which are as fundamental to development in art as they are to other subject areas. Nevertheless, because the average child's potential in art is underdeveloped, the gap between the backward child's achievement and that of the normal child is not always as apparent as in reading or arithmetic; nor, since art is not usually subject to examination and assessment, is the less able child's lack of success made so obvious to him. In general the backward child is a defeated child as far as most school work is concerned, and he is therefore desperately in need of success in some field. If school cannot provide this need, then the child looks for it elsewhere, and the older the pupil becomes the more this may be found in fields which are antipathetic, if not actually opposed, to what the school is attempting to achieve. The turning away from school and what it stands for is one of the most fundamental problems facing teachers of adolescents, and although the causes of this are complex, a major factor is the continued failure of the less able child in the activities which are at the core of the school's existence.

More able children, as they approach the early teens, can sustain effort in pursuit of long term goals and indeed will begin to question the value of activities such as art, which have no immediately obvious advantage in job-getting. The less able child has little patience with activities which do not offer him immediate reward in some form or other – and enjoyment of the activity itself is the most effective form of reward. The activities of arts and crafts which have been discussed in this book, because they are always concrete activities which involve hands and body as well in the mind, because they offer physical challenge, because they offer

tactile sensation and pleasure, because many of them are direct and immediate in their response to a child's action, are able to capture and maintain his interest and enthusiasm. It is this which makes them so valuable for the teacher of backward children, for such activities can be the basis on which new relationships with the children can be built, and the basis upon which they may be steered into new successes in other areas of learning.

Any class of children seems to have one or two who acquire a name for 'being good at art'. When this is analysed it usually means having a natural ability for realistic drawing. When it occurs it is a gift to be developed, but the peculiarity of this particular talent is the effect it has on other pupils, for the work of such gifted children is apt to be taken as the standard to which all others should aspire. When this occurs in a group of backward children the effect is apt to be even more critical. It is important therefore for the teacher to introduce activities which call on abilities far wider than this particular ability to draw well.

All that has been written about the various aspects of art and craft in this book can be applied to working with backward children. However, many teachers rely far too much on painting with backward children. As a very direct expressive activity it lacks the direction and clear cut stages offered by many of the crafts. Indeed, because painting is flexible and allows for wide interpretation the child may be quite undermined by the wide range of possibilities offered. Some things therefore should be underlined as being especially suitable for them and certain methods can be more effective than others.

One of the most impressive experiences that one of the authors has had was with boys of around thirteen who became involved in carving in wood and alabaster and building in plaster on mild steel armatures (skeletons).

The boys were in the lower ability range of a very large school and not very easy to handle. Fortunately it was possible to work with them in an old concrete hut well away from other buildings where both noise and mess did not cause a nuisance to other classes. The two main materials – wood and alabaster – were obtained cheaply as offcuts and provided irregular lumps ranging from about 150 mm × 100 mm × 75 mm (6 in. × 4 in. × 3 in.) to three or four times these dimensions. The irregular lumps of stone or wood often suggested the form which could be developed. Sometimes a visit was made to the local museum to study the animals on display, from which the boys returned with ideas of various animals they might carve. They then searched for a piece of alabaster or wood which came nearest to the form they had in mind. Carving is a process which is vigorous in its early stages and satisfyingly noisy, and the boys enjoyed the physical activity. As the work progressed, more skill was developed and greater care was demanded by the nature of the job; it was interesting to see the increasingly careful control exercised by the boys as the form began to emerge. Finally, and most impressively, great care was taken over the final finish of the work, and boys who were not noted for careful work in other subjects would spend hours working with 'wet and dry' abrasive paper to bring a beautiful surface to their carving. Alabaster was particularly rewarding in this respect although the wood too received the same careful attention. Sand paper was avoided and surfaces were obtained by careful scraping with fragments of broken glass. The children were sensitive to the difference between the surface obtained in this way which has a clean 'cut' quality in comparison to the floury quality of a glass-papered surface – and to obtain this degree of discrimination is an important achievement (see figures 77–81).

Some of the boys also worked with plaster of paris on armatures of mild steel rod set in blocks of plaster. The bending and wiring together of the basic form were again a physical challenge, and the mixing and pouring of the plaster into boxes in which the armatures were set had a sense of crisis which gave pupils and teacher a feeling of shared achievement. The scale of the work was fairly large – perhaps 1 m (3¼ ft) or so in height, and the models were given bulk by the addition of chicken wire, blocks of wood,

77 Carving in wood by a thirteen year old boy

cardboard boxes, rolls of paper – anything in fact which could be held in place by rag or paper dipped in plaster. The forms created included animals and birds and the human figure, and although they sometimes began from a starting point in the museum there was a tendency for the idea to change as the developing model suggested new possibilities – or even sometimes as it went wrong and had to be changed. Indeed, the capacity to change first ideas and seize on new possibilities is one of the by-products of this type of working.

These activities have been described in some detail because they illustrate a number of important principles of working with less able children and especially those approaching the early teens. These are:

a   provide the children with a scale of work which will give them a real sense of challenge and achievement
b   provide them with materials which offer a physical challenge and an outlet for their abundant energy
c   provide a process which begins 'rough' and allows the child to develop more skill and finesse as the job progresses
d   provide a process which does not invite an habitual response.

Other principles are illustrated by some work undertaken with a very backward group of thirteen year old boys and girls who were the fifteenth stream in a comprehensive school. These children were not only backward but many of them displayed problems of social maladjustment and other psychological characteristics which made the group a very difficult class to handle. The most successful work done with this group was a series of lino prints using the elimination process in which each colour is printed successively from the same block. The children were pathetically lacking in confidence and they were allowed to base their lino-cuts on photographs from newspapers. Their grasp of the process was not very clear and they needed careful guidance through each step, but over a period of two or three weeks each of them was able to bring a lino-cut through to a three colour print and finish up with several good prints. As a final process they were helped to cut simple 'window mounts' from appropriately coloured papers and mount up a couple of prints. They showed great delight in their success and clearly they had had little previous experience of success in any sphere at all.

The important points here are:

a   the carrying through of the project to a successful stage
b   the careful nursing through each stage of the job
c   the willingness to allow children to take whatever was possible as a starting point
d   the turning of this into a more creative process by the 'translation' from black and white into imagined colour.

Children who learn slowly are going to need much more help in early stages of a process and may need to proceed in simple steps before they can be asked to explore on their own. If freedom has to be learned, then the more backward a child is the more difficult it will be for him to acquire freedom of action, for his own inner resources are that much more limited. In print-making for example, he will probably need to be shown mono-printing techniques one at a time and allowed to practice each one before proceeding to the next, whereas a more able child could be shown the principle and allowed to explore the process freely himself.

The less able child is necessarily more teacher dependant than his more able classmate, yet at the same time as he grows into young adolescence, possibly more resistant to what the teacher has to offer. One of the advantages of the various activities that have been described is that the materials and processes themselves attract and involve the children in a satisfying way and at the same time impose a discipline upon them, for success is dependant on some technical skill and effort.

Younger children are less likely to be streamed off in the way the children were in the two instances discussed previously, and teachers most often have to cope with an ability range which includes some children with high IQ's at one end and others bordering on ESN at the other. These latter children are often frustrated and bored and immature in their response to materials. Again they need work of such a scale that it requires a full physical response. Clay, for example, should be provided in large quantities – perhaps the trays provided in infant classes for water and sand play could be adapted for use with clay so that two or three hundredweight of clay is available for children to use freely as they wish. When not in use the clay could be covered over with a wet sack and a polythene sheet. Paint and cheap paper needs to be large in scale, and perhaps in some schools a wall could be found which could be set aside for children to draw and paint on. The emphasis is on the process of drawing and painting and not on the finished product.

Simple pattern making with vegetable blocks or found objects can also be a rewarding activity for the less able children. If it is approached as a rhythmic printing process, particularly if ink pads, which simplify the process of inking the block, are used a child can achieve a result quickly and easily and can be encouraged to further control and complexity. Children are helped by 'rules of the game', and these could be to make a pattern that grew from the centre or to make a pattern which was in stripes. Simple pattern can be very satisfying and much primitive pattern work is extremely simple, although subtleties occur through the rhythmic process of printing. Children can be encouraged by seeing examples of such pattern, and their origin on clubs, shields, canoes, wigwams and the like might add further interest and lead out into other areas of work. Collage, too, using units such as seeds, berries, bottle tops, shells or chippings offers the child an activity which may have some element of repetition, but also has a high degree of flexibility and allows for exploration and development over long periods of time.

The danger in working with less able children lies in the temptation to help them too much. They are already inclined to be teacher-dependant and the teacher must be careful only to give sufficient help to ensure success, and carefully nurture the child's own moves towards taking responsibility for his own work. When asked by the child what he should do next, the teacher should try to show *two*

possible courses of action so that the child is forced into making a choice. Even where the question is related to a purely technical matter, as for example in making a colour lino-cut, it should still be possible to suggest alternative developments; for example 'If you want this bit to stay red cut it out with the gouge and then try printing in two colours'. The ability to make choices can only be developed if the children's experiences are structured so that they are choosing between alternatives that they understand. If the children are slow learners then the choice must be simplified.

It is obvious that working in this way has a therapautic effect for children who have difficulty in learning and for whom school offers little satisfaction. There are those who would claim a therapautic value for art at any level and there is truth in this claim. Although one would hesitate to justify art in the curriculum on these grounds alone, there is no doubt that for backward children art plays this valuable therapautic role. Any situation which can provide a child with a feeling of success and builds his self-confidence is bound to be beneficial. Coupled with such achievement is the possibility of building new relationships between the teacher and the child.

78, 79 Carvings in wood and alabaster
by thirteen year old boys

80, 81 Carvings in alabaster by thirteen year old boys

APPENDIX 1

A simple process for making black and white slides

Equipment
Simple safelight: Paterson's or similar, or an improvised safelight, eg a cycle rear-light.
3 dishes capable of taking lengths of film about 254 mm (10 in.) long; these need not be photographic dishes and could be improvised from food containers as used for deep-freezers or for packing picnic food.
A plastic washing-up bowl, a wash-basin or sink.
Two pieces of glass about 35 mm (1⅜ in.) by 280 mm (11 in.); these can be cut quite cheaply by any glass merchant.
Small hand towel or paper towels.

Materials
Positive film: This is best obtained through the advertisement pages of magazines, such as *The Amateur Photographer*, and can be bought very cheaply.
Developer: This should be either a Universal Developer or a High Contrast Developer. Johnsons make both of these types.
Fixative: This can be bought as a liquid or a powder; the latter is probably a little cheaper but the liquid form is the most convenient to use.

This process can be carried out in any darkened room and does not need the meticulous elimination of cracks of light around doors since the positive film used is not particularly sensitive to light. However, chinks of daylight coming from an inefficiently blacked out window could be disastrous, and if this problem cannot be solved, the only way out is to work after dark. At home the kitchen or bathroom would make suitable workrooms at night, in school a windowless stockroom would probably serve very well for daytime use.

Positive film is sensitive to orange or red light only, and it is quite safe to handle in the light from a photographic safelight or from a red torch or cycle lamp. It must not be taken out of its packet or tin in ordinary room light or it will be ruined.

Procedure

1

Mix up enough developer according to the instructions on the bottle to give about 12 mm (½ in.) depth in the smallest dish which should be long enough to take about 254 mm (10 in.) of film. Fill a second dish with plain cold water. Mix up sufficient quantity of fixative to give about 25 mm (1 in.) depth in the third dish. The dilutions for different makes of chemicals vary but generally speaking developer is diluted about 1 to 7 and fixative much the same, although a stronger solution will speed up the process. Ideally the temperature should be around 68 degrees farenheit but this is not critical. In winter if the water from the cold tap seems very cold it might be as well to add a little warm water but for most of the year the water in the cold tap will not be far out in temperature. Unless a sink is handy it is also necessary to have a washing-up bowl or a bucket of cold water.

2

When the solutions are prepared and set out in line from left to right on a table or bench, prepare a place to deal with the film. This can be on the same bench but it must not be close enough for there to be a danger of getting splashes of chemical or water on the working space. Ideally another work-bench should be used. On this dry work area place the negatives from which slides are to be made, the two pieces of glass, the positive film still wrapped-up inside its container, scissors and an anti-static cloth such as is used to wipe records. The safelight should be in a position where it can illuminate both working areas.

3

Switch out the main light, leaving only the safelight on. Unwrap the positive film and cut off a length just slightly longer than six frames of the negatives (if these are shop-developed they will probably have already been cut into sixes). Re-wrap the film and return it to its container. Sandwich the positive film and the negatives' emulsion (dull) sides together between the two strips of glass with the negatives uppermost. With the sandwich on the bench and the positive film safely returned to its container, switch on the main illumination and count two, so that for two seconds the film is exposed to light shining *through* the negatives with which it is in close contact.

4

Take the exposed strip of film and slide it into the developer. In about a minute it should be possible to see the image appear and by about two minutes it should be fully developed. With the hand that has developer on it, pick the film out of the developer and drop it into the second dish. With the other hand, pick the film out of the water and drop it into the fixative. Wait for a couple of minutes until the milkiness in the film disappears and then switch the light on. If the print is very pale the exposure must be lengthened, if it is very dark or all black the exposure must be shortened or the strength of the light changed.

Light sources vary according to the wattage of the bulb, the distance from the workbench, whether they are shaded or not, and so it is not possible to give any real idea of what is correct exposure. Longer exposures are much easier to control than short ones and it would be better to change a 100 watt bulb for a 40 watt, for example, than struggle to get consistent exposures with the more powerful bulb. A small reading lamp used for the exposures makes control easy in that it can be moved away to avoid a direct light on the film. It may be necessary to make a number of trials before a satisfactory print is obtained. Once the correct exposure has been established this can be used for all the rest of the negatives unless they vary greatly in density and contrast. Should this be so then new trials will have to be made for each change.

5

Having established the correct exposure, print from all the negatives in the way described. When the first one has been in the fixative for ten minutes it can be taken out and put in the bowl of water or the sink. The final process is washing to remove all the chemicals. The usual advice is to wash for one hour in running water or to use twelve changes of water. If permanance is not particularly important and the slides will not be wanted after a few days or weeks it is not necessary to carry out this washing process quite so conscientiously. When the prints are ready to dry off they should be taken out of the water and as much as possible shaken off. They can then be hung up on a line with clothes pegs or alternatively held upright on their long edge on newspaper by clothes pegs each end. Avoid putting wet prints in a dusty atmosphere and handle with great care or they will collect scratches.

6

When dry the prints are cut up and mounted in card slide mounts and are ready for projection. It is worth while marking the mount with an arrow or a spot at the top right hand corner to indicate which way up it should be put in the projecter. Most people find this is best done when they have established the correct way by trial and error in the projector.

Problems

The greatest problem in this process is created by dust. Any spot of dust or minute piece of fluff between the glass or the two films will cause white marks. It can help if the glass and the negatives are wiped with an anti-static cloth before they are sandwiched together and it is advisable to work on a dust free surface – formica or a clean sheet of drawing paper, for example.

Marks may also appear from spots of water which remained on the film during drying and leave a water-mark when they eventually evaporate. A tiny spot of detergent in the final wash water may help to get rid of this problem.

APPENDIX 2

List of art materials, tools, etc.

Drawing and painting
Paints and colour media

Powder colours
Offer experience of colour mixing or can be made into liquid colour by adding water. Brilliant colour – non smearing. Varying degrees of opacity may be obtained. Some firms market two grades – only the best is worth having.

Ready mixed colours
May be used spontaneously without the preliminary stage of colour mixing. They have good covering power and may be used on a wide range of surfaces. Particularly good for working on models, masks, puppets, etc.

PVA colours
Stands for polyvinyl acetate. May be used thickly or in thin glazes. Dry as a tough waterproof film. May be used on a variety of surfaces including cardboard, plastic, newspaper, wood and canvas.

PVA medium
Mixed with powder colour, it provides better handling characteristics and dries with a waterproof sheen.

Acrylic colours
Expensive. Thick consistency – one may achieve the high impasto quality of oil paint. Can be used on a variety of surfaces. Dry rapidly.

Tempera blocks
Quick to issue and collect. Little waste, but may be frustrating for children to use because of the effort involved in obtaining sufficient colour.

Designers colours
Expensive, but may be used for detailed small scale work, where a high degree of finish may be obtained. They have exceptional opacity.

Poster colours
Supplied in paste form. May be used as an alternative to powder colour. Brilliant colours, with excellent matt covering power. Can be purchased in bulk for dispensing in smaller quantities.

Water colours
Transparent and delicate washes may be achieved. No longer so widely used but they offer children the chance to produce subtle, sensitive work. Tube colour is easier to use than colour in pans.

Oil colours
Expensive. Little used in the classroom. No other pigment, however, offers the opportunity to achieve such a wide range of colour and tonal effects.

Waterproof drawing inks
Transparent, but more brilliant than watercolour. May be used with a brush or a pan. Fairly expensive, but worth having for occasional use.

Brusho colours
Very cheap, transparent colour. Obtainable in small drums of powder to make up into one pint quantities.

Pastels
Made from pigments ground with a mixture of chalk, clay and other ingredients. They are soft and have a velvety texture in use. If work is to be preserved they will require fixing.

Oil pastels
Provide both an oil and a pastel effect. They do not require the use of a fixative.

Wax crayons

Inexpensive. The large sized crayons are easily gripped by young children. Many pre-school children however find it difficult to obtain sufficient pressure to make satisfactory marks.

Felt topped markers   (*Spirit based*)

These are indelible. They produce bright colours easily, but are expensive.

Felt tipped markers   (*Water colour*)

Produce brilliant colours. Easy to use, best for small scale work. Expensive.

Fibre tipped pens

Excellent for drawing, particularly for older children. May be used in conjunction with water colours, pastel, etc.

Coloured pencils

Not a very suitable tool for producing areas of colour.

Chalks   (*Coloured*)

Inexpensive. Soft, and therefore very suitable for young children to use.

Ball point pens

Useful for drawing out of doors. Inexpensive, long lasting.

Brushes

Ox ear hair brushes   (*Pointed*)

Inexpensive, hard wearing. Have more spring than squirrel or ringcat, and will outlast them many times. Ideal for use with inks, water colour or colour cakes.

White bristle fitch brushes   (*Flat or round*)

Long lasting, inexpensive. Ideal for use with powder, poster or ready mixed colours. Size 8 is probably the most useful size.

Nylon brushes   (*Flat or round*)

Very hard wearing, and have good colour holding properties. Ideally suited for a wide range of art and craft activities.

Housepainters brushes

12 mm ($\frac{1}{2}$ in.) and 25 mm (1 in.) sizes are particularly useful for covering large areas. Inexpensive, compared to 'art' brushes of similar sizes.

Papers

Newsprint

Similar to kitchen paper. Inexpensive. May often be obtained from a local printer. Has a wide use for experimental work and is especially useful for printing. Will not stand up to very wet paint.

Sugar paper

Absorbent. The most suitable paper for painting with powder, or ready mixed colours. Will stand up to vigorous handling.

Cartridge papers

May be obtained in sheets or in continuous rolls. Expensive. Hard and non absorbent. Excellent for pen or pencil drawing, or work with water colours or inks.

Art cover papers

(Coloured cartridge paper.) Useful range of subtle colours. Takes paint well. Suitable for printing and for mounting work.

Glazed coloured paper (*Gummed back*)

Strident colours. Perhaps used more than they should be.

Coloured tissue papers

Wide and subtle range of colours. Suitable for a variety of purposes including printing.

Duplicating paper

Inexpensive. Very suitable for drawing. Not many different sizes.

Collage

Adhesives

Cellulose paste (*Polycell, Gloycell, etc*)
Only suitable for sticking papers.

Cellulose 'heavy duty' paste
Suitable for thicker papers, card, vinyl papers, thin fabrics, and polystyrene.

Marvin medium, PVA medium **and similar binders**
Wood, seeds, sand and other materials embedded in the surface will stick firmly in position. Dry transparent.

Gloy Multi-glue
Good general purpose adhesive. May be used for sticking a wide variety of materials, from bottle tops to pieces of wood. Dries transparent.

Contact adhesives (*Evostik, Bostik, etc*)
Essential for securing large scale or heavy materials.

Backgrounds

Papers
A variety of thick papers or card are suitable for bases for use with thin materials in low relief (eg papers, fabrics).

Cardboard
Pieces of thick brown card, obtainable from cardboard boxes, provide an excellent foundation for a range of collage materials.

Strawboard
Supplied in a number of thicknesses; it provides a first class ground for all but the heaviest materials.

Hardboard
Ideal for work with junk-yard scrap, and other heavy gauge materials. Offcuts may be obtained at reasonable cost from builders merchants.

Plywood, chipboard, blockboard
A range of backgrounds such as these are very suitable if offcuts can be obtained at reasonable cost.

Printing

Colours

Block printing colours (*Water*)
Ideal for work with children over a wide age range. Suitable for mono, vegetable, junk, block or lino printing.

Block printing colours (*Oil*)
Give a higher degree of finish than water based colours, but are messy, difficult to clean and the resultant prints take a long time to dry.

Screen printing inks (*Oil or cellulose based*)
Expensive. Give excellent results. These are best obtained from specialist firms.

Fabric printing pigment dyestuffs
Suitable for screen and block printing on paper or fabric. Mixed with a suitable medium will produce transparent colours. Colours are water soluble and equipment may be washed in water.

Cold water paste and dyes
Can be used as an improvised screen ink.

Tools and equipment

Rollers
Rubber covered. Buy the widest with the largest diameter that you can afford.

Foam rollers
Useful in place of a squeegee for screen printing. Many objects with irregular surfaces can be 'inked up' with them for block printing.

Squeegees
For fabric printing, strips of wood or card can be used if a blanket is placed underneath the fabric. For graphic printing using a hard printing surface a rubber squeegee is required.

Lino tools (*Gouges*)
The common nib tool is dangerous and tends to break easily. It is better policy to buy wood cutting gouges.

Fabric for making screens
Organdie, although not as fine as silk, is suitable and far cheaper.

Improvised materials
For rolling out a film of ink, a number of flat smooth surfaces may be used. Old mirrors, glass, glazed ceramic tiles, plastic or decorative laminates are all suitable for this purpose.

Work with image producing materials

Carving

Materials

Materials
Reference should be made to the text. See page 57.

Adhesives
Reference should be made to the list in the appendix (see *Collage*, page 89).

Miscellaneous
In addition, a variety of sizes of panel pins, oval and round wire, nails, staples, screws and thin binding wire will be required.

Tools
A suitable collection of tools which will have wide application in the art room should include hammers, pliers, pincers, handsaws, coping saws, chisels, mallets, screwdrivers, bradawls, wire cutters, hand drills, bench hooks, vices, scissors, Stanley knives and a staple gun.

It is desirable to have at least one carpenter's work bench.

Materials

Salt
Blocks of salt, which are still widely obtainable (some supermarkets stock them), are useful for beginners. They are very soft and may be carved with a blunt knife.

Soap
Inexpensive green washing soap is good for sensitive small scale carving. May be carved with penknives, nailfiles and lino cutters.

Unfired (green) bricks
These cheese-hard bricks can be obtained from a local brickworks, and they provide an excellent carving material. Because the material is fairly soft, some of the residual clay can be used for developing the 'carved' model by using a modelling technique. The models can be fired after completion.

Thermal insulation blocks
Used in the building trade for the construction of non-load bearing inside walls; they are suitable for medium scale carving. The material is fairly soft and relatively inexpensive. Broken blocks may be obtained from builders merchants, for little cost. May be shaped easily with rasps.

Pre-set plaster of Paris
Irregular and interesting carving blocks may be produced by pouring the wet plaster mixture into polythene bags. Rectangular blocks may be obtained by pouring the wet plaster into cardboard boxes. Cheap industrial plaster should be used.

Fire bricks
Obtainable from some brickworks or builders merchants. They are lightweight, open grained and soft, and can be carved with a penknife.

Wood

A variety of woods may be used, but it is important to offer materials which can be carved readily with the tools available. Hardwood is more satisfactory to use than soft wood but requires sharp tools.

Alabaster

A beautiful material for carving, and can be brought to a highly polished surface. Best carved with rasps to avoid fracturing the material. Can sometimes be purchased as off-cuts from monumental masons.

Stone

Some local stones may be suitable for work with older children. It is essential to obtain relatively soft stone.

Polystyrene

May be bought in sheet or block form but tends to be expensive. Waste polystyrene used for packing may often be obtained from stores.

Tools

Rasps

Stone and wood rasps, useful for rough work.

Files

They clog easily, but are useful in the final stages of the work.

Chisels and gouges (*Wood*)

Special tools can be obtained but children can work successfully with carpenters tools.

Chisels and gouges (*Stone*)

Mallet-headed tools should be obtained from specialist suppliers.

Surform

Useful general purpose tool for shaping wood, stone, etc.

Coping saws

Good, all round tool for a variety of cutting purposes, with wood and soft carving materials.

Hot wire cutters

A specialist tool for cutting polystyrene. The smaller version tends to break.

Vices

Carpenter's or engineer's vices can be used but require padding with cloth to prevent the work from being damaged or bruised.

Improvised tools

12 mm (6 in.) nails

Can be flattened and sharpened to a chisel-end, for carving stone and thermal insulation blocks.

Clamps

A variety of clamps may be used successfully for securing the work.

Sandbox

Stone and Thermal Insulation blocks can be bedded in boxes of sand to steady them for carving. This also helps to deaden the noise.

Plastic materials

Plasticine

For effective use to be made of this material, it should be provided in substantial quantities.

Clay

Best bought locally, if it can be obtained, to avoid carriage costs. Red clay is more suitable than white for work that is to be fired and gives a pleasing result. Brickworks may supply a local brick clay suitable for modelling.

Storage

For information on storing clay reference should be made to specialist books.

Firing

Firing can be carried out in simple kilns, such as sawdust kilns, which the children can construct. For information on firing, reference should be made to specialist books.

BIBLIOGRAPHY

History of Art

W Gaunt, *A Concise History of English Painting*, Thames and Hudson London, Praeger New York, 1964

E M Gombrich, *The Story of Art*, Phaidon London

H Read, *A Concise History of Modern Painting*, Thames and Hudson London, Praeger New York, 1959

H Read, *A Concise History of Modern Sculpture*, Thames and Hudson London, Praeger New York, 1964

Drawing and Painting

R Capon, *Introducing Drawing Techniques*, Batsford London, Taplinger New York, 1974

F Gore, *Painting: Some Basic Principles*, Studio Vista London, 1965

E Hill, *The Language of Drawing*, Prentice Hall New Jersey and London, 1966

E Röttger, *Creative Drawing: Point and Line*, Batsford London, Van Nostrand Reinhold New York, 1964

K Rowland, *Learning to See, Book 1 and Teacher's Book (Design in the Primary School)*, Ginn London, 1964

K Rowland, *Looking and Seeing, Books 1 and 2 and Teacher's Book (Design in the Secondary School)*, Ginn London, 1964

University of Bristol, School of Education, *Coloured Things, Stages 1 and 2*, Macdonald London, 1970 (Schools Council Publications)

Collage and Embroidery

A Butler and D Green, *Pattern and Embroidery*, Batsford London, Branford Newton Centre, 1970

M Conner, *Introducing Fabric Collage*, Batsford London, Watson-Guptill New York, 1969

N d'Arbeloff, *Creating in Collage*, Studio Vista London, Watson-Guptill New York, 1967

R Hartung, *Colour and Texture in Creative Textile Craft*, Batsford London, Van Nostrand Reinhold New York, 1964

R Hartung, *Thread and Fibre: Creative Textile Craft*, Batsford London, Van Nostrand Reinhold New York, 1964

C Howard, *Inspiration for Embroidery*, Batsford London, Branford Newton Centre, 1967

E John, *Filling Stitches*, Batsford London, 1967

F Kay, *Starting Fabric Collage*, Studio Vista London, Watson-Guptill New York, 1969

E Mason, *Embroidery Design*, Mills and Boon London, 1968

M Thomas, *Mary Thomas's Dictionary of Embroidery Stitches*, Hodder and Stoughton London, 1952

A Timmins, *Making Fabric Wall Hangings*, Batsford London, Watson-Guptill New York, 1970

Printing

J R Biggs, *Woodcuts*, Blandford London, 1963

H Curwen, *Printing*, Penguin Harmondsworth, n e

P Green, *Introducing Surface Printing*, Batsford London, Watson-Guptill New York, 1967

C Kent and M Cooper, *Simple Print-making*, Studio Vista London, Watson-Guptill New York, 1966

A Kinsey, *Introducing Screen Printing*, Batsford London, Watson-Guptill New York, 1967

J Newick, *Making Colour Prints*, Dryad London, 1964

J O'Connor, *Introducing Relief Printing*, Batsford London, Watson-Guptill New York, 1973

M Rothenstein, *Lino-cuts and Wood-cuts*, Studio Vista London, 1962

M Rothenstein, *Frontiers of Print-making*, Studio Vista London, 1966

Constructions and Carving

C Jarman, *Woodwork with Young Children*, Batsford London, Van Nostrand Reinhold New York, 1974

J Porchmouth, *Creative Crafts for Today*, Studio Vista London, Viking New York, 1969

J Mills, *The Technique of Sculpture*, Batsford London, 1965

H M Percy, *New Materials in Sculpture*, Tiranti London, 1962

E Rogers and T Sutcliffe, *Introducing Constructional Art*, Batsford London, Watson-Guptill New York, 1970

Claywork

M Cardew, *Pioneer Pottery*, Longmans London, 1971

D Cowley, *Working with Clay and Plaster*, Batsford London, Watson-Guptill New York, 1973

W Farnworth, *Clay in the Primary School*, Batsford London, Van Nostrand Reinhold New York, 1973

D Green, *Experimenting with Pottery*, Faber London, 1971

D Green, *Pottery: Materials and Techniques*, Faber London, 1971

D Green, *Understanding Pottery Glazes*, Faber London, 1963

J Newick, *Clay and Terracotta in Education*, Dryad London, 1964

S M Robertson, *Beginning at the Beginning with Clay*, S E A Pamphlet, 1965

E Röttger, *Creative Clay Craft*, Batsford London, Van Nostrand Reinhold New York, 1963

Mosaics

J Berry, *Making Mosaics*, Studio Vista London, Watson-Guptill New York, 1966

A Garnett, *Mosaics*, Oxford University Press, London and New York, 1967

H Unger, *Practical Mosaics*, Studio Vista London, 1965

Film Strips

Changing the Face of Things, 6 filmstrips compiled and annotated by John S Beswick. Particularly relevant to work on colour, they include sections on the effect of pattern and colour, reflections and light, camouflage and display.

Looking at Things, 8 filmstrips compiled and annotated by Nigel Temple. A course in design for Secondary Schools.

Both sets obtainable from Visual Publications, 197 Kensington High Street, London W8

SUPPLIERS

General Art and Craft Materials

E J Arnold Ltd (School Suppliers)
Butterley Street, Leeds LS10 1AX

Brodie and Middleton Ltd
79 Long Acre, London WC2

Dryad Ltd
Northgate, Leicester

J B Duckett
Broadfield Street, Sheffield

Margros Ltd
Monument House
Monument Way West
Woking, Surrey

Reeves and Sons Ltd
Enfield, Middlesex

George Rowney and Co Ltd
10-11 Percy Street, London W1

Winsor and Newton Ltd
Wealdstone
Harrow, Middlesex

Papers and Cards, etc

English Corrugated Paper Co Ltd
Portland Street, Bristol

Hunt and Broadhurst Ltd
Botley Road, Oxford

F G Kettle
127 High Holborn, London WC1

Miconite
Blackhorse Lane, Walthamstow

Milburn Clifford and Co Ltd
54 Fleet Street, London EC4

Paperchase Products Ltd
216 Tottenham Court Road,
London W1

Reed Corrugated Card
Towville, Bristol

Printing Equipment

A G W Britten and Sons Ltd
Shenton Street, Old Kent Road
London SE15

George Hall Ltd
11 Wellington Road
Stockport, Lancashire

John T Keep and Sons Ltd
Victoria Paint Works
15 Theobalds Road, London WC1

Screen Process Supplies Ltd
24 Parsons Green Lane, London SW6

Clay

Chelsea Pottery
13 Radnor Walk, London SW3

Fremington Clays Ltd
Fremington, Devon

Fulham Pottery
210 New King's Road, London SW6

Mills and Hubbard Ltd
Victoria Rise
Clapham, London SW4

Moira Clay Company
Moira, Staffordshire

Podmore and Sons Ltd
Shetlon, Stoke-on-Trent

Potclays Ltd
Copeland Street, Stoke-on-Trent

Watts Blake and Bearne and Co Ltd
Newton Abbot, Devon

Wengers Ltd
Etruria, Stoke-on-Trent
Staffordshire

Clay is costly to transport and should be obtained locally if possible. Small potteries, brickworks, tile or pipe manufacturers, fireplace makers for example may be prepared to supply good clay at reasonable prices. These clays often have more 'character' than the very plastic clays supplied for pottery and are excellent for hand-built work.

Carving and Modelling

Tiranti Ltd
72 Charlotte Street, London W1

Shearman and Co Ltd
Vicarage Road, Abbotskerswell
Newton Abbot, Devon

Stone and timber for carving are best obtained locally – Monumental Masons will sometimes supply small pieces of suitable stone or suggest sources locally. Country timber yards can often supply suitable woods for carving which are not normally available from large yards concentrating on imported timber. Fruit woods, lime and beech are particularly suitable if they can be obtained.